AMERICA REDUX

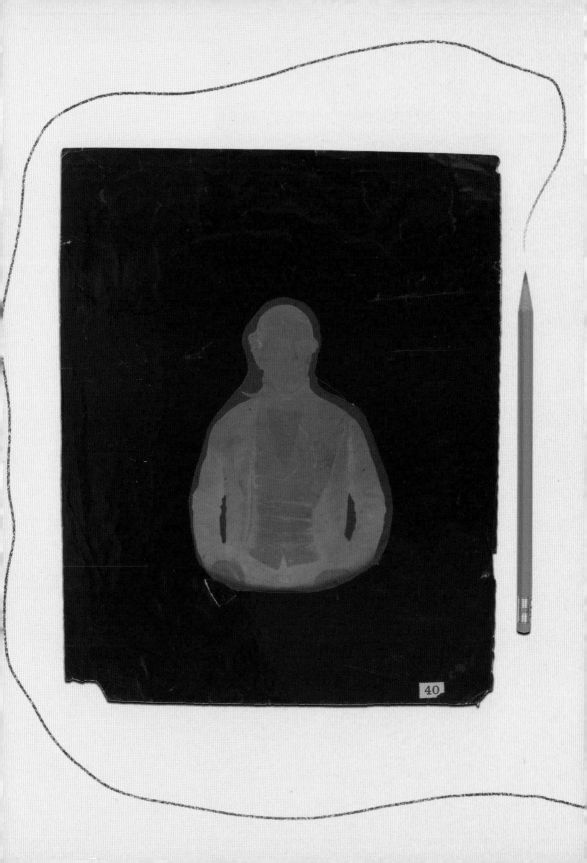

AMERICA REDUX

VISUAL STORIES FROM OUR DYNAMIC HISTORY

ARIEL ABERG-RIGER

BALZER + BRAY
An Imprint of HarperCollinsPublishers

The collage art for this book was created using Photoshop and Procreate.

Original typography for text created in Calligraphr by Ariel Aberg-Riger.

Parts of the following chapters have been previously published in
different forms: "White Picket Fences," "Made in America,"
"Nose to the Grindstone," and "We the People" with CityLab;
"Down on the Farm" on *TeenVogue*.com.

24 25 26 27 28 COS 10 9 8 7 6 5 4 3 2 1

First paperback edition, 2024

TO YOU

**YOU HAVE MORE POWER
THAN YOU KNOW.**

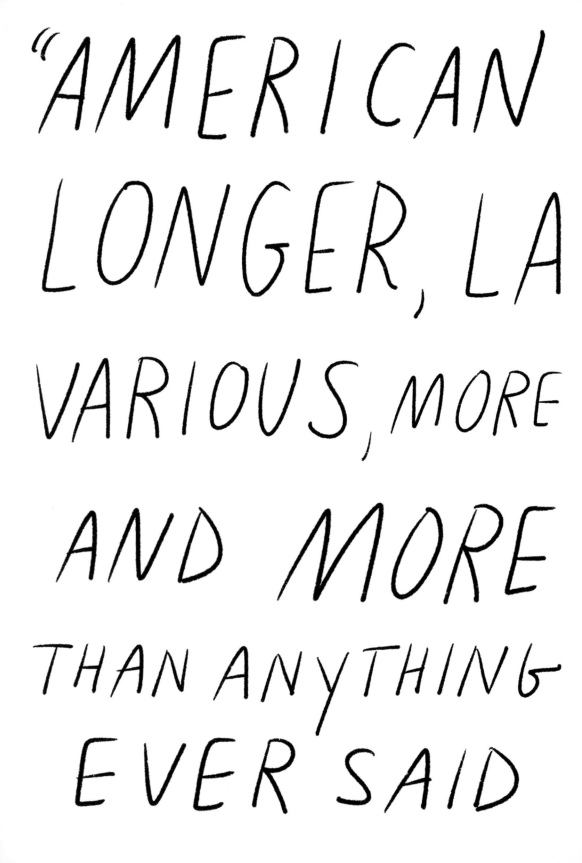

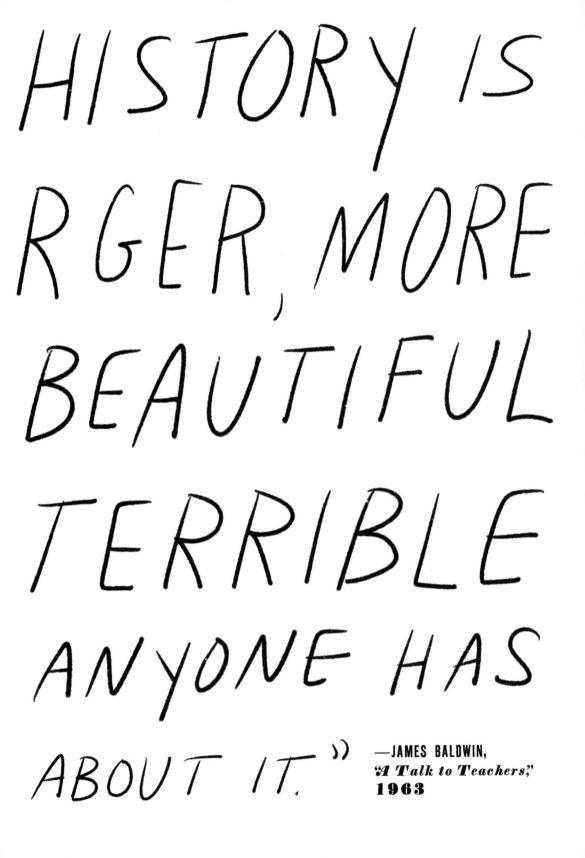

CONTENTS

PREFACE 1

THE GOOD
OLD DAYS 7

LET FREEDOM
RING 21

SPREADING
DEMOCRACY 35

A NATION OF
IMMIGRANTS 47

TRADITIONAL
FAMILY VALUES 57

ONE NATION
UNDER GOD 69

HOME OF
THE BRAVE 83

GIVE ME
LIBERTY 99

GOOD GUY
WITH A GUN 109

A NEW
WORLD 123

THIS LAND
IS YOUR LAND
133

A CAR IN
EVERY GARAGE
149

WHITE
PICKET FENCES
161

WISH YOU
WERE HERE
177

AS AMERICAN
AS
191

THE OLD
BALLGAME
203

DOWN ON
THE FARM
213

MADE IN
AMERICA
225

STREETS PAVED
WITH GOLD
237

NOSE TO THE
GRINDSTONE
247

WE THE
PEOPLE
257

AFTERWORD
ACKNOWLEDGMENTS
IMAGE SOURCES
SELECTED BIBLIOGRAPHY
INDEX
267

PREFACE

One of my favorite books when I was younger was a big book called *The Wall Chart of World History*. It had a musty-colored, marbled cover and looked like the kind of thing you'd find in someone's attic steam trunk, the kind of thing that might magically spit you back into the Mesopotamian desert if you weren't careful. The wall chart was a visual timeline that started in 4004 BCE and stacked the histories of people and civilizations from all over the world on top of one another in wavy colored streams. The pages were all connected, folded in on themselves so that you could accordion them out into a giant strip. When the whole thing was unfurled, it was longer than my bedroom. I'd lie on my stomach and follow the streams with my fingers, watching colored bands bloat and shrivel as nations ate each other up or slowly died away.

The book, it turns out, was an expanded reproduction of the *Adams' Synchronological Chart of Universal History—Through the Eye to the Mind* made by Sebastian C. Adams in 1871. Adams was a white Christian missionary whose belief in Manifest Destiny drove him across the Oregon Trail in the nineteenth century. His "universal" chart is very him—it starts with Adam and Eve, celebrates Eurocentric history, and is dominated by white men (even the cavemen are pale).

But it's not just *who* he chooses to feature that's limited by his own world-view, it's *how* he chooses to visualize the notion of time itself. In Adams's world, time is a line, a stream that moves in one direction—from the past to the present. A stream might have multiple branches, but all are parallel, rushing along neatly segmented years, forward, forward, never to return.

Had Adams delved into histories and philosophies beyond his own, he would have found that many cultures and communities (including many Native nations living right next to him in Oregon) didn't conceive of time as a line at all.

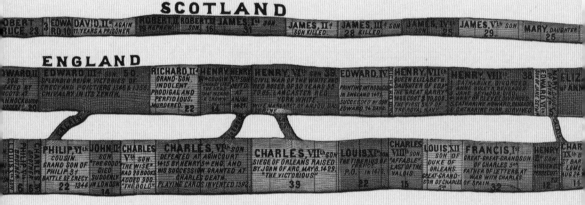

Instead, time was seen as it was experienced, as a cycle—day to night to day, spring to summer to fall to winter to spring, generations upon generations of babies to adults to elders and back again.

Notions of nonlinear time crop up everywhere from the Mayans to the Celts, Chinese thought to classical Indian philosophy, African conceptions to Diné traditions. There is a kaleidoscope of philosophies, all with their own interpretations and variations, but one thing that comes up again and again is the belief that time is a continual, ever-evolving *relationship*, not a series of isolated, fixed points on a line.

Native ethnohistorian Donald Fixico writes about Native American conceptions of time and notes that the linear mind "looks for cause and effect," while the "Indian mind seeks to comprehend relationships." The emphasis is on achieving balance—within yourself, your family, your community,

broader communities, the environment—not endlessly hurtling away from the past toward some future progress.

As a white American brought up on deadlines and timelines and dots and dates, I've been bound to a boat on the river of time, rushing forward for as long as I can remember. I was taught to memorize history when I had to. I was raised to look back on it at a distance.

It wasn't until I was well into my thirties that I fell into a relationship with history, and it happened through images. I began searching historical archives for photographs and objects and artifacts I could collage into my art, and they called me in. I found myself wanting to know more about who the people in the portraits were. I wanted to know their stories.

It made me wish that I could've explored history more visually when I was younger. A history textbook is so impersonal. The type, the layout, the tone. Its design intentionally makes the subject feel distant. I love visual storytelling because the opposite is true. Visual storytelling is a form and a framework that tweaks your brain into seeing differently and reading differently and digesting information differently. It's not just the image that matters, but how it takes up space. It's not just the event that matters, but how we shape the stories around it.

This book is nothing like the history textbooks I grew up with. It's visual, it's handwritten, it jumps around in time. It's an attempt at a new way of seeing history—placing movements and events and people from across time in conversation with one another in a way that, I hope, offers some insight into who we are as a country, and who we have the power to become.

I've tried to achieve a small ecosystem of balance by including a number of different time periods and people and themes. It's wildly incomplete, the beginning of a beginning. But that's the point. If you, like me, like to learn this way, I hope it gives you just enough to start seeing history around you all the time—in the placement of the freeways near your home, in the expressions you hear again and again, in the images we use as shorthand for "America."

Forms change us, and I hope this book changes you. A poem has the ability to shape us into the truth just as much as (if not much more so than) a list of facts. I hope you question these stories, this book. I hope your questions turn into creation—of conversation, of art, of action.

BECAUSE
HISTORY IS NOW.
HISTORY IS YOU.
HISTORY IS A
RELATIONSHIP
THAT NEVER
ENDS...

THE GOOD OLD DAYS

AT TWO A.M. ON THE LAST DAY OF MAY 2020,
FLAMES POURED FROM THE HEADQUARTERS OF THE
UNITED DAUGHTERS OF THE CONFEDERACY.
IGNITED BY PROTESTORS DURING THE
UPRISINGS FOR RACIAL JUSTICE, THE
BLAZE WAS QUICKLY PUT OUT,
BUT THE MESSAGE WAS
CLEAR:

WE KNOW
WHO YOU ARE,
AND WE KNOW
WHAT YOU
DID.

THE END OF THE CIVIL WAR
LEFT WHITE SOUTHERNERS DEJECTED.

WOMEN WERE WIDOWED AND LEFT CHILDLESS. OTHERS WATCHED
AS THEIR SONS, BROTHERS, FATHERS, AND HUSBANDS
RETURNED HOME IN DEFEAT.

THEY BELIEVED THESE CONFEDERATE MEN WERE HEROES AND WANTED
TO HONOR THEIR SERVICE. SO THE GROUPS AFFLUENT WHITE WOMEN HAD
FORMED DURING THE WAR TO SEW UNIFORMS AND NURSE THE WOUNDED
GREW INTO ASSOCIATIONS TO CARE FOR VETERANS AND
COMMEMORATE THE DEAD.

BY THE LATE 1800S, THOSE SMALLER WOMEN'S
ASSOCIATIONS BEGAN BANDING TOGETHER, AND IN 1894,
THE UNITED DAUGHTERS OF THE CONFEDERACY
WAS FORMED.

IT HAD BEEN THREE DECADES SINCE THE END OF THE CIVIL WAR,
THREE DECADES SINCE THE PRACTICE OF WHITE PEOPLE ENSLAVING BLACK PEOPLE
HAD BEEN OUTLAWED.

IN THAT TIME, DURING A PERIOD KNOWN AS RECONSTRUCTION,
BLACK PEOPLE HAD FOUGHT FOR AND WON SIGNIFICANT GAINS—
US CITIZENSHIP, DUE PROCESS AND EQUAL PROTECTION UNDER
FEDERAL LAW, THE RIGHT FOR BLACK MEN TO VOTE,
SEATS IN LOCAL AND NATIONAL LEGISLATURES.

WHITE SOUTHERNERS DID NOT
RESPOND WELL TO THESE GAINS.

THEY USED SUSTAINED CAMPAIGNS OF
RACIAL TERROR—
BLACK CODES, THE KU KLUX KLAN,
PUBLIC SPECTACLE LYNCHINGS—
TO ENSURE THAT THE RIGHTS BLACK PEOPLE
HAD SECURED WERE IN NAME ONLY, AND
COULD NOT BE EXERCISED FULLY.

IT WAS INTO THIS ERA OF RENEWED, EMBOLDENED
WHITE POWER THAT THE UNITED DAUGHTERS
OF THE CONFEDERACY WAS BORN.

A NEW WHITE SOUTHERN GENERATION WAS
COMING OF AGE, AND IT WANTED
VINDICATION.

THE WAR HAD BEEN LOST,
BUT ITS LEGACY COULD STILL BE WON.

THE DAUGHTERS WEAPONIZED THEIR STATUS AS
WEALTHY WHITE WOMEN INTO AN

ARMY OF INFLUENCE.

THEY WROTE LETTERS AND RAISED MONEY AND LOBBIED
LOCAL OFFICIALS. THEY ERECTED MONUMENTS TO THE HEROES
OF THE CONFEDERACY, ENSURING THAT JEFFERSON DAVIS AND
"STONEWALL" JACKSON AND ROBERT E. LEE TOWERED OVER AS MANY
TOWN HALLS, COURTHOUSES, AND PUBLIC PARKS AS POSSIBLE.

MAMIE GARVIN FIELDS, A BLACK TEACHER AND ACTIVIST, WROTE IN HER MEMOIRS ABOUT HOW MUCH BLACK PEOPLE **DETESTED** THE UDC'S MONUMENTS, HOW CLEARLY AND VISCERALLY THEY UNDERSTOOD THEM TO BE A WAY OF WHITE PEOPLE TELLING BLACK PEOPLE TO **STAY IN THEIR PLACE.**

WHEN THE UDC ERECTED A STATUE OF **JOHN C. CALHOUN**— A POLITICIAN AND SLAVER WHO SAW SLAVERY AS A **"POSITIVE GOOD"**— IN CHARLESTON, SOUTH CAROLINA, BLACK RESIDENTS **THREW ROCKS** AT IT AND DEFACED IT EVERY CHANCE THEY GOT.

BUT WHITE WOMEN FLOCKED TO THE UDC'S MISSION AND ACTIVITIES.

BY WORLD WAR I, UDC MEMBERSHIP HAD **BALLOONED TO NEARLY 100,000** IN CHAPTERS FAR BEYOND THE SOUTH, FROM **NEW YORK TO INDIANA TO CALIFORNIA.**

THE DAUGHTERS DIDN'T STOP AT PHYSICAL MONUMENTS. THEY WANTED SOMETHING THAT WOULD ENDURE GENERATION TO GENERATION, SO THEY BEGAN CRAFTING A

"LIVING MONUMENT"—

IN THEIR CHILDREN.

THEY RAISED THEIR CHILDREN IN THE CULTURE OF THE "LOST CAUSE," WHERE PLANTATION OWNERS WERE KIND CARETAKERS OF SLAVES UNEQUIPPED TO HANDLE FREEDOM.

THE LOST CAUSE DEPICTED SLAVERY AS A BENEVOLENT INSTITUTION INTEGRAL TO SOUTHERN CULTURE, AND TO ITS ADHERENTS, THE "WAR BETWEEN THE STATES" WASN'T ABOUT SLAVERY, BUT CULTURAL DIFFERENCES BETWEEN THE NORTH AND THE SOUTH.

THE CONDITIONING WAS JOYFUL.

IT GAVE WHITE CHILDREN PRIDE IN THEIR FAMILIES, AND IN THEIR SOUTHERN HERITAGE.

ONCE THEIR OWN CHILDREN HAD BEEN INDOCTRINATED, THE DAUGHTERS MOVED TO INDOCTRINATE OTHER PEOPLE'S CHILDREN AS WELL,

THROUGH TEXTBOOKS.

IN 1919,
MILDRED LEWIS RUTHERFORD, THE HISTORIAN
GENERAL OF THE UDC, CREATED "A MEASURING ROD,"
A PAMPHLET THAT LAID OUT THE DOS AND DON'TS OF WHAT SHOULD BE
INCLUDED IN CHILDREN'S TEXTBOOKS. IF A BOOK DIDN'T MEASURE UP, MOMS AND
TEACHERS AND LIBRARIANS WERE INSTRUCTED TO PULL IT FROM THE SHELVES,

WRITE "UNJUST TO THE SOUTH"

ON THE COVER, AND REFUSE TO TEACH IT.

Breakfast In A Plantation Home

115

THE EFFORT WAS
INCREDIBLY SUCCESSFUL.

THE UDC GOT TEXTBOOKS BANNED AND
TEACHERS FIRED. ITS INFLUENCE SHAPED
THE WAY GENERATIONS OF CHILDREN
LEARNED ABOUT AMERICAN HISTORY
WELL INTO THE 1970S.

THE 1961 EDITION OF
KNOW ALABAMA,
THE ALABAMA STATE BOARD-APPROVED HISTORY
TEXTBOOK, DESCRIBES THE KU KLUX KLAN AS

The loyal white men of Alabama

AND PLANTATION LIFE AS

one of the happiest ways of life in Alabama before

the War Between the States.

FOURTH-GRADE READERS ARE ASKED TO IMAGINE
A DAY IN THE LIFE ON A beautiful
PLANTATION WHERE THEIR FATHER IS THE Master
AND THEIR MOTHER IS THE mistress . IT'S A WORLD
WHERE, YES, THERE WERE SLAVES, BUT
Most of them were treated kindly
AND THE MISTRESS IS THE
best friend the Negroes have .

THE CHAPTER IS WRITTEN ENTIRELY IN
THE SECOND PERSON

You wake up   You eat   you ride   You play

ENCOURAGING CHILDREN TO STEP INTO
THE STORY AND EXPERIENCE DELICIOUS
MEALS OF FRIED HAM AND SWEET BISCUITS,
PRETTY HORSES, NAPS IN BIG
BEDROOMS, AND
LOVELY PARTIES,

ALL WHILE
ENSLAVED
PEOPLE
SMILE AND
WAVE IN
THE
BACKGROUND.

NOT ONLY WHITE CHILDREN WERE BEING
TAUGHT FROM THESE TEXTBOOKS.

BLACK CHILDREN WERE AS WELL.

BLACK ADULTS PUSHED BACK FOR OVER 100 YEARS,
FROM THE 1870S TO THE 1970S.

LEADERS FROM FREDERICK DOUGLASS TO W. E. B. DU BOIS
WERE OUTSPOKEN ON THE NEED TO COMBAT A

WHITE SUPREMACIST TELLING OF HISTORY.

AND BLACK ADVOCACY GROUPS FROM THE NAACP TO THE
NATIONAL URBAN LEAGUE TO THE CONGRESS OF RACIAL EQUALITY
TO THE BLACK PANTHER PARTY FOR SELF-DEFENSE

RAILED AGAINST RACIST TEXTBOOKS,

URGING SCHOOL BOARDS AND CITIES TO CHANGE THEM.

IT WASN'T JUST IN THE SOUTH.

NORTHERN TEXTBOOKS WERE LESS OVERTLY RACIST AND
REVISIONIST, BUT STILL SOAKED IN WHITE SUPREMACY—
HISTORY TEXTBOOKS SYMPATHETIC TO SLAVERS, GEOGRAPHY
TEXTBOOKS CELEBRATING COLONIALISM, BIOLOGY TEXTBOOKS
REINFORCING THEORIES OF RACIAL HIERARCHY.

WHEN THE NAACP PUSHED WHITE, NORTHERN, LIBERAL
OFFICIALS IN CITIES LIKE ALBANY AND CHICAGO TO

REMOVE THE MOST HATEFUL PASSAGES
FROM LOCAL TEXTBOOKS IN THE 1940S,

OFFICIALS DISMISSED THEIR APPEALS, WITH SOME
ATTRIBUTING THE OBJECTIONS TO "HYPERSENSITIVITY."

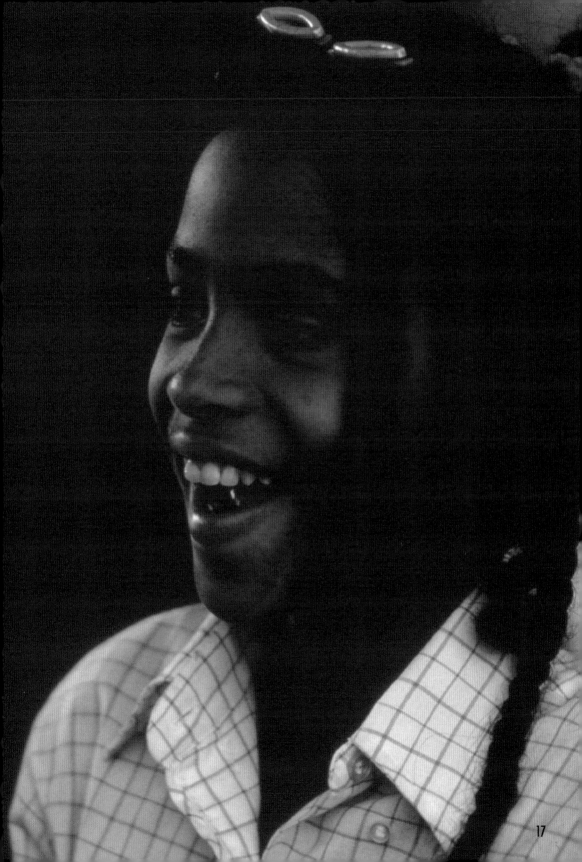

BUT WHAT NORTHERN WHITES FAILED TO GRASP WAS THAT THE CHANGES WEREN'T JUST FOR THE FEELINGS OF BLACK CHILDREN. THEY WERE FOR THE

HUMANITY OF WHITE CHILDREN.

WHITE CHILDREN WHO INTERNALIZE HISTORY AS BEING

WRITTEN BY WHITE PEOPLE, STARRING WHITE PEOPLE, FOR WHITE PEOPLE.

TODAY, THE STRUGGLE TO CONTROL THE HISTORICAL NARRATIVE CONTINUES.

THERE IS A GROWING LEGISLATIVE MOVEMENT THAT AIMS TO RESTRICT HOW SCHOOLS CAN TEACH STUDENTS ABOUT RACE AND SYSTEMIC RACISM, WITH 563 MEASURES INTRODUCED IN 2021 AND 2022 ALONE.

THE LAWS ARE OFTEN SWEEPING AND VAGUE, LEADING TEACHERS TO CUT LESSONS, DISCUSSIONS, AND TEXTS FOR FEAR OF REPRISAL. IN ONE CASE A TEACHER IN IOWA WAS TOLD THEY COULD NO LONGER TEACH STUDENTS THAT "SLAVERY WAS WRONG" BECAUSE IT IS CONSIDERED A STANCE, NOT A FACT.

SOME LAWMAKERS ARE EVEN SEEKING LEGISLATION TO REMOVE ENTIRE WORDS AND CONCEPTS FROM CLASSROOMS, SUCH AS "EQUITY," "ANTI-RACISM," AND "OPPRESSOR VS. OPPRESSED."

BOOK CHALLENGES AND BANS HAVE ALSO INCREASED SHARPLY, DRIVEN BY HIGHLY POLITICIZED GROUPS LIKE MOMS FOR LIBERTY WHICH ENCOURAGE PARENTS TO PULL BOOKS FROM SCHOOL LIBRARY SHELVES USING TACTICS THAT ECHO THOSE OF THE UDC.

A SINGLE BRAVE PERSON LIKE BREE NEWSOME CAN CLIMB A STATEHOUSE FLAGPOLE AND REMOVE A CONFEDERATE FLAG. BUT ONCE ERECTED, LIVING MONUMENTS ARE MUCH MORE DIFFICULT TO TAKE DOWN.

BETWEEN 1889 AND 1969, 69,706,756 STUDENTS WERE ENROLLED IN PUBLIC SCHOOLS IN THE SOUTH—NEARLY 70 MILLION CHILDREN HOLDING A HISTORY IN THEIR HEARTS AND THEIR HEADS THAT A GROUP OF WHITE WOMEN SIMPLY MADE UP.

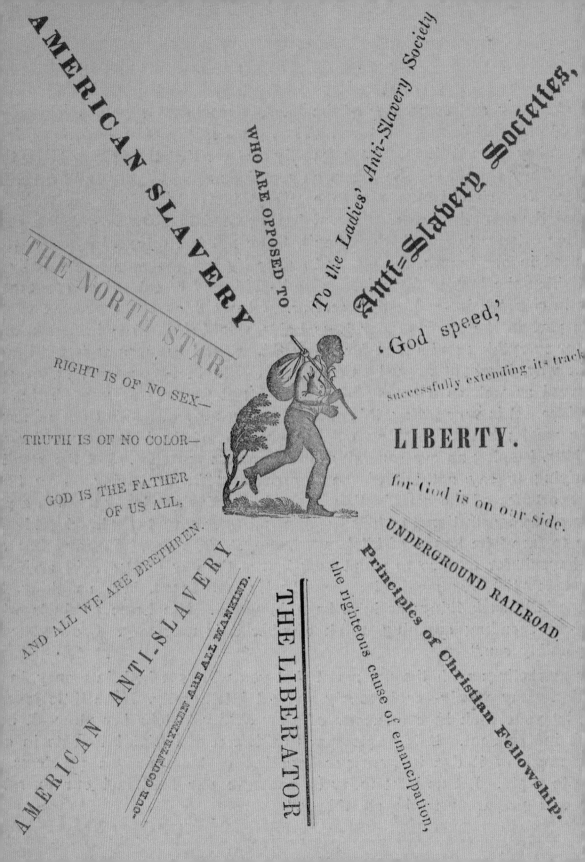

AMERICAN SLAVERY

WHO ARE OPPOSED TO

To the Ladies' Anti-Slavery Society

Anti-Slavery Societies,

THE NORTH STAR

RIGHT IS OF NO SEX—

TRUTH IS OF NO COLOR—

GOD IS THE FATHER OF US ALL,

AND ALL WE ARE BRETHREN.

'God speed,'

successfully extending its track

LIBERTY.

for God is on our side.

UNDERGROUND RAILROAD.

Principles of Christian Fellowship.

the righteous cause of emancipation,

THE LIBERATOR

AMERICAN ANTI-SLAVERY

OUR COUNTRYMEN ARE ALL MANKIND.

LET FREEDOM RING

IN THE 1820S, THERE WERE STILL

NUMEROUS NATIVE NATIONS

EAST OF THE MISSISSIPPI DESPITE HUNDREDS OF YEARS OF SETTLER VIOLENCE AND EUROPEAN DISEASE THREATENING THEIR SURVIVAL.

WHEN ANDREW JACKSON BECAME PRESIDENT IN 1829,

HE WAS DETERMINED TO CHANGE THAT.

JACKSON WANTED NATIVE LANDS FOR THE GROWING UNITED STATES, AND HE SOUGHT TO USE HIS PRESIDENTIAL POWER TO TAKE THEM. THE SUPREME COURT RULED THAT HE HAD NO JURISDICTION TO DO SO—THE LAND BELONGED TO OTHER NATIONS— BUT JACKSON PUSHED THE INDIAN REMOVAL ACT THROUGH CONGRESS IN 1830.

HE CLAIMED THE ACT GAVE HIM THE POWER TO FORCIBLY REMOVE THE SEMINOLE, MUSCOGEE (CREEK), CHOCTAW, CHICKASAW, AND CHEROKEE FROM THEIR HOMES ACROSS THE SOUTHEAST. CONGRESSMEN FROM SLAVEHOLDING STATES BACKED HIM UP, BECAUSE THEY KNEW THAT IF NATIVE PEOPLE WERE REMOVED, THEIR NATIVE LANDS— VAST, FERTILE TRACTS OF LAND— COULD BE DIVVIED UP AND SOLD TO WHITE AMERICAN INVESTORS AND PLANTERS ON THE CHEAP.

BY 1835—JUST FIVE YEARS LATER—SOUTHERN PLANTATIONS WERE PRODUCING MORE COTTON ON THOSE STOLEN LANDS THAN ALL THE OTHER COUNTRIES IN THE WORLD COMBINED.

IT WAS WILDLY LUCRATIVE.

COTTON MADE UP MORE THAN HALF THE VALUE OF ALL U.S. EXPORTS AND FUELED THE GROWTH OF BUSINESSES IN THE NORTH, FROM TEXTILE FACTORIES TO INSURANCE COMPANIES.

THE INSTITUTION OF SLAVERY HAD BEEN DECLINING IN THE LATE 18TH CENTURY, BUT BY THE 1830s, THANKS TO COTTON, IT WAS ON AN UPSWING.

ONE IN THIRTEEN AMERICANS— ALMOST ONE MILLION PEOPLE—GREW COTTON, AND NEARLY ALL OF THEM WERE

ENSLAVED.

SLAVERY WAS A BRUTAL, VIOLENT ECONOMIC SYSTEM AND THE BLACK PEOPLE WHO WERE EXPLOITED AND TORTURED BY WHITE PLANTERS TO MAINTAIN IT **ACTIVELY RESISTED ITS HORROR.**

ENSLAVED PEOPLE ORGANIZED WORK SLOWDOWNS, MISPLACED AND BROKE EQUIPMENT, PRETENDED TO BE SICK, PRODUCED SHODDY WORK, STOLE FOOD AND TOOLS AND FABRIC, SET THINGS ON FIRE, DESTROYED CROPS, GOT MARRIED WITHOUT SLAVEHOLDERS' PERMISSION, FOUND WAYS TO EDUCATE THEMSELVES, AND—

DESPITE THE DANGER—
ATTEMPTED TO ESCAPE THEIR CAPTORS.

THOSE WHO ESCAPED OFTEN TRIED TO FIND REFUGE IN THE NORTH, JOINING ESTABLISHED COMMUNITIES OF FREE BLACK PEOPLE IN CITIES LIKE PHILADELPHIA, NEW YORK, AND BOSTON, AND FINDING SUPPORT IN A SMALL BUT GROWING GROUP OF **ABOLITIONIST ALLIES.**

ABOLITIONISTS WERE
BOUND TOGETHER
IN THEIR BELIEF THAT SLAVERY
SHOULD BE ABOLISHED, BUT THEY
WERE A DIVERSE GROUP WITH
DIVERSE OPINIONS ABOUT HOW TO
FIGHT THE SYSTEM
MOST EFFECTIVELY,
AND HOW BEST TO
AID THOSE
BEING BRUTALIZED BY IT.

SOME BELIEVED IN
GRADUAL ABOLITION,
WHILE OTHERS CALLED FOR
THE INSTITUTION'S
IMMEDIATE END.
SOME BELIEVED IN USING
NONVIOLENT APPROACHES,
WHILE OTHERS BELIEVED A VIOLENT SYSTEM
CALLED FOR **VIOLENT RESISTANCE.**

SOME THOUGHT THE FOCUS
SHOULD BE ON CONVERTING
WHITE PEOPLE TO THE ANTI-
SLAVERY CAUSE, WHILE OTHERS
BELIEVED THAT OFFERING
**MATERIAL AID TO THE
BLACK PEOPLE HARMED**
BY SLAVERY WAS OF THE
UTMOST
IMPORTANCE.

F'S SALE.

executions issued by the Clerk of
Andrew County, Mo., and to
e Shultz
e th Davis
2434 00 dollars and
day of March April
house door is Savannah Mo
t bill at public outcry, all the
said George W Davis
scribed personal property, to-wit:

ned Martin aged 71 years,
med Walker aged 33 years
ned Rachel aged 37 years
ned Amanda aged 11 years,
ned Alice aged 6 years
ned Polly aged 8 years
named Addie aged 8 years
want to satisfy said Execution
th March 15th 1862
want Ferfull Sheriff
Andrew County Mo April

FREE BLACK PEOPLE—BOTH BORN FREE AND FORMERLY ENSLAVED—
DROVE THE ABOLITIONIST MOVEMENT,
DEVELOPING SURVIVAL NETWORKS AT GREAT COST
TO THEMSELVES, TO EXTEND THEIR OWN
TENUOUS FREEDOM TO OTHERS.

SELF-EMANCIPATION WAS HARROWING—
THOSE ESCAPING HAD NO HOME, NO MONEY, NO IDEA WHO TO TRUST,
AND WERE CONSTANTLY HUNTED BY WHITE KIDNAPPERS AND THE POLICE.

WHEN FREDERICK DOUGLASS FLED TO NEW YORK CITY IN 1838,
HE WAS TOLD TO FIND DAVID RUGGLES, A CONDUCTOR ON
THE UNDERGROUND RAILROAD AND ORGANIZER OF THE NEW YORK
COMMITTEE OF VIGILANCE. THE GROUP TOOK UP ARMS
TO CONFRONT SLAVE CATCHERS, PASSIONATELY ADVOCATED FOR BLACK
PEOPLE IN COURT, AND PROVIDED AN ARRAY OF RELIEF INCLUDING
SHELTER, FOOD, COMMUNITY, ADVICE, TRANSPORTATION, AND
ACTIVISM EDUCATION. RUGGLES CALLED IT
"PRACTICAL ABOLITION,"
AND BY THE 1840S, THERE WERE VIGILANCE
COMMITTEES ACROSS THE NORTHEAST.

BLACK ABOLITIONISTS USED THEIR SKILLS TO DO WHATEVER THEY COULD.

THEY WROTE:

DAVID WALKER'S APPEAL URGED THE ENSLAVED TO VIOLENTLY RESIST THEIR CAPTIVITY.

THEY SPOKE:

FREDERICK DOUGLASS MOVED LISTENERS TO TAKE ACTION VIA POWERFUL TESTIMONIES.

THEY SANG:

ELIZABETH TAYLOR GREENFIELD—A WORLD-RENOWNED ARTIST—SHATTERED STEREOTYPES AND SANG ON THE ABOLITIONIST LECTURE CIRCUIT.

THEY FUNDRAISED:

WOMEN BAKED, SEWED, AND CRAFTED, POOLING AND COLLECTING MONEY.

THEY PROTECTED:

MANY USED THEIR HOMES, CHURCHES, AND BUSINESSES AS SAFE HAVENS.

THEY ABETTED:

OTHERS ARMED THEMSELVES WITH EVERYTHING FROM GUNS TO POTS OF BOILING WATER TO RUN OFF PRO-SLAVERY FORCES.

27

WHITE PEOPLE—OF ALL CLASSES—
ALSO JOINED THE MOVEMENT,
USING THEIR ACCESS

TO POWER

TO DRAW ATTENTION
TO THE ANTI-SLAVERY
CAUSE AND ENCOURAGE
OTHER WHITE PEOPLE
TO FOLLOW SUIT.

THE GRIMKÉ SISTERS USED THEIR
STATUS AND EXPERIENCE AS SOUTH CAROLINIAN
WHITE WOMEN RAISED BY SLAVERS TO SPREAD
AWARENESS ABOUT THE HORRORS OF SLAVERY.

WILLIAM LLOYD GARRISON LAUNCHED A WEEKLY
ANTI-SLAVERY NEWSPAPER,

THE LIBERATOR,

TO ELEVATE ABOLITIONIST VOICES.

CHARLES TURNER TORREY FORMED THE BOSTON
VIGILANCE COMMITTEE, WORKED TO AID 400 PEOPLE
AS THEY FREED THEMSELVES, AND FOUNDED

THE LIBERTY PARTY

(WHOSE SOLE PLATFORM
WAS ABOLITION).

HE WAS A MAJOR
SOURCE OF
INSPIRATION FOR

JOHN BROWN,

THE RADICAL WHITE ABOLITIONIST WHO
DEDICATED HIS LIFE TO OVERTHROWING
SLAVERY, LEADING NUMEROUS
VIOLENT RAIDS AGAINST SLAVERS,
INCLUDING THE RAID AT HARPERS FERRY—
A CATALYST FOR THE CIVIL WAR.

BUT WHILE WHITE ABOLITIONISTS LIKE TORREY AND BROWN **WORKED IN CONCERT** WITH BLACK ABOLITIONISTS, OTHER WHITE ABOLITIONISTS DIDN'T WANT BLACK PEOPLE TO BE PART OF THEIR ABOLITIONIST ORGANIZING AT ALL.

SOME WHITE ABOLITIONISTS, EVEN WHILE CALLING FOR THE END OF SLAVERY, SAW BLACK PEOPLE AS INFERIOR, AND **DIDN'T BELIEVE IN FULL EQUALITY.**

SOME BELIEVED THAT AMERICA WASN'T A PLACE FOR FREE BLACK PEOPLE, AND THAT THEY SHOULD BE COLONIZED TO AFRICA TO **LEAVE THE COUNTRY WHITE.**

RESISTANCE TO THE MACHINERY OF SLAVERY WAS
A DANGEROUS BUSINESS—
AND THE REACTION FROM PRO-SLAVERY FORCES
TO ABOLITIONIST ORGANIZING WAS FIERCE.

THE AMERICAN ANTI-SLAVERY SOCIETY'S MEETINGS
AND LECTURES WERE ROUTINELY MET WITH

MOB VIOLENCE—

THE GROUP'S FIRST ANNIVERSARY
MEETING IN NEW YORK CITY
IN 1834 CAUSED A

THREE-DAY
RIOT.

FIGHTING THE MOB IN INDIANA.

ABOLITIONISTS WERE FREQUENTLY
JAILED, BEATEN, HARASSED, AND KILLED
BY PRO-SLAVERY FORCES SUCH AS POLICE DEPARTMENTS
WHO WORKED IN CONCERT WITH KIDNAPPERS AND SLAVE CATCHERS.
AND LIVING SUCH AN EMOTIONALLY AND PHYSICALLY DEMANDING LIFE
HAD CORROSIVE EFFECTS. DAVID RUGGLES DIED AT THIRTY-NINE AFTER
YEARS OF FAILING HEALTH AND RECURRENT BLINDNESS. CHARLES
TURNER TORREY DIED OF TUBERCULOSIS IN PRISON. JOHN BROWN
BECAME THE FIRST PERSON TO BE EXECUTED FOR TREASON
BY THE UNITED STATES GOVERNMENT.

ON THE EVE OF THE CIVIL WAR,
THE VAST, LUCRATIVE MACHINERY OF SLAVERY SEEMED STRONGER THAN EVER.

IN 1860, THERE WERE **FOUR MILLION ENSLAVED** PEOPLE ESTIMATED TO HAVE BEEN WORTH AT LEAST **$3 BILLION—** MORE THAN ALL THE CAPITAL INVESTED IN RAILROADS AND FACTORIES COMBINED.

DURING THE **CIVIL WAR,** ABOLITIONISTS JOINED FORCES WITH THE UNION ARMY.

SOJOURNER TRUTH RECRUITED BLACK TROOPS TO ENLIST, AND **HARRIET TUBMAN** GATHERED INTELLIGENCE, AIDED SELF-EMANCIPATED PEOPLE IN "CONTRABAND" CAMPS, AND **COMMANDED A BATTLESHIP** DOWN THE COMBAHEE RIVER, **FREEING 750 PEOPLE** IN ONE FELL SWOOP.

SLAVERY OFFICIALLY ENDED OVER 150 YEARS AGO, BUT THERE ARE STILL ABOLITIONISTS FIGHTING TODAY TO ABOLISH OTHER **SYSTEMS THAT CONTINUE TO BRUTALIZE** BLACK PEOPLE, SUCH AS **PRISONS** AND THE **POLICE.**

TWENTY-FIRST-CENTURY ABOLITIONISTS NOTE THAT POLICING IN THE SOUTH GREW OUT OF THE **SLAVE PATROLS** THAT CAPTURED RUNAWAY SLAVES, AND THAT THE CONTEMPORARY CARCERAL PUNISHMENT SYSTEM CAN BE TRACED BACK TO SLAVERY AS WELL.

"THE CHALLENGE OF THE TWENTY-FIRST CENTURY IS NOT TO DEMAND EQUAL OPPORTUNITY TO **PARTICIPATE IN THE MACHINERY OF OPPRESSION,**" ABOLITIONIST **ANGELA DAVIS** WRITES, "RATHER, IT IS TO **IDENTIFY** AND **DISMANTLE** THOSE STRUCTURES IN WHICH RACISM CONTINUES TO BE **EMBEDDED.**"

SPREADING DEMOCRACY

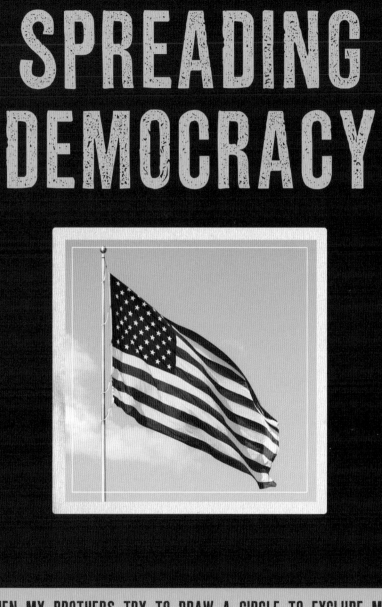

"WHEN MY BROTHERS TRY TO DRAW A CIRCLE TO EXCLUDE ME,
I SHALL DRAW A LARGER CIRCLE TO INCLUDE THEM."

—PAULI MURRAY

IN THE EARLY 1830S, WHEN ABOLITIONIST MEN WOULDN'T LET WOMEN JOIN THEIR ANTI-SLAVERY SOCIETIES, **WOMEN BEGAN TO FORM THEIR OWN.** ALTHOUGH THEIR FIGHT WAS FOR ABOLITION, THEY WERE ALSO—JUST BY THE SHEER FACT OF BEING WOMEN PUSHING FOR SOCIAL AND POLITICAL AGENCY AND CHANGE—

FIGHTING FOR GENDER EQUALITY.

THE RIGHTS OF AMERICAN WOMEN AT THE TIME VARIED DRAMATICALLY BASED ON THE STATE THEY LIVED IN, THEIR RACE, THEIR CLASS, THEIR MARITAL STATUS.

BUT ACROSS THE BOARD WOMEN DID NOT HAVE THE SAME RIGHTS AS MEN, AND THEY COULDN'T VOTE.

ALTHOUGH THIS IMBALANCED POWER STRUCTURE WAS A NORM FOR EUROPEANS AND AMERICANS, THERE WERE PLENTY OF WOMEN AT THE TIME WHO KNEW A VASTLY MORE LIBERATED EXPERIENCE.

HAUDENOSAUNEE WOMEN,

CITIZENS OF THE SIX NATIONS CONFEDERACY (SENECA, CAYUGA, ONONDAGA, ONEIDA, MOHAWK, AND TUSCARORA), WERE NEIGHBORS TO SOME OF THE MOST FAMOUS ABOLITIONISTS AND WOMEN'S RIGHTS ACTIVISTS.

THEY WERE HIGHLY RESPECTED IN THEIR SOCIETIES (WHICH WERE MATRILINEAL), THEY HAD A POWERFUL ROLE IN GUIDING GOVERNANCE AND COULD HOLD POLITICAL OFFICE THEMSELVES, AND THEY CONTROLLED PROPERTY AND HAD BODILY AUTONOMY.

THEY ALSO HAD A DIRECT EFFECT ON AMERICAN WOMEN'S RIGHTS ACTIVISTS, WHO WIDENED THEIR VISION OF WHAT AN EGALITARIAN SOCIETY COULD BE BY LEARNING FROM THE WAY HAUDENOSAUNEE WOMEN LIVED.

AS THE 19TH CENTURY PROGRESSED, THE AMERICAN WOMEN'S RIGHTS MOVEMENT GAINED MOMENTUM, GROWING OUT OF THE ABOLITIONIST MOVEMENT TO BECOME ITS OWN FERVENT CAUSE.

INDIGENOUS WOMEN DID NOT BENEFIT FROM THAT EXPANSION.

IN FACT, THROUGHOUT THE 19TH CENTURY NATIVE WOMEN DEVASTATINGLY LOST RIGHTS AS THE U.S. GOVERNMENT DISPLACED THEIR NATIONS AND FORCED THEM TO ASSIMILATE INTO AMERICAN SOCIETY.

DURING THE 1848 SENECA FALLS CONVENTION,
SEEN AS THE FIRST WOMEN'S RIGHTS CONVENTION,
ORGANIZER ELIZABETH CADY STANTON READ

THE DECLARATION OF SENTIMENTS,

WHICH OUTLINED SIXTEEN WAYS IN WHICH WOMEN WERE TREATED
INFERIOR TO MEN, AND DEMANDED CHANGE.

THE DEMANDS REFLECTED THE LIVED EXPERIENCES
OF THE WOMEN WHO WROTE THEM—

WHITE, MIDDLE-CLASS, MARRIED WOMEN.

THEY WERE FOCUSED ON THE LOSS OF RIGHTS, WEALTH, AND PROPERTY
IN MARRIAGE, AS WELL AS LIMITATIONS ON HIGHER EDUCATION.

NO BLACK WOMEN WERE PRESENT AT THE CONVENTION, AND WORKING-CLASS WOMEN WERE LARGELY ABSENT,

EVEN THOUGH MOST WORKERS AT TEXTILE MILLS WERE WOMEN,
AND THE LOWELL "MILL GIRLS" HAD BEEN ORGANIZING FOR
THEIR OWN RIGHTS FOR MORE THAN TWENTY YEARS.

THE DECLARATION OF SENTIMENTS DIDN'T FOCUS ON
SLAVERY IN THE SOUTH, NOR FACTORY CONDITIONS IN THE NORTH—
BOTH OF WHICH GREATLY AFFECTED MILLIONS OF AMERICAN WOMEN.

AS BLACK FEMINIST FRANCES ELLEN WATKINS HARPER
PUT IT PLAINLY AT A SUFFRAGE CONVENTION IN 1866,

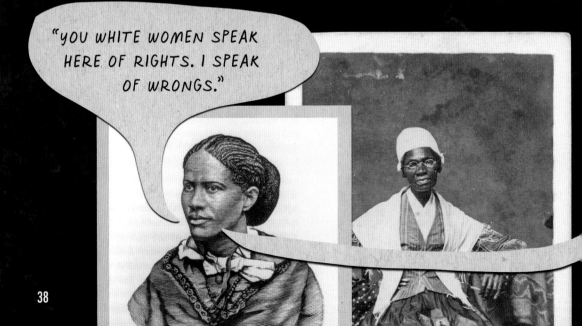

"YOU WHITE WOMEN SPEAK
HERE OF RIGHTS. I SPEAK
OF WRONGS."

THESE DIFFERENCES WERE BROUGHT INTO SHARP RELIEF AFTER THE CIVIL WAR WHEN THE QUESTION OF BLACK MEN GAINING THE RIGHT TO VOTE WAS RAISED.

LEADING WHITE FEMINISTS LIKE STANTON AND SUSAN B. ANTHONY WERE INCENSED THAT BLACK MEN WOULD ACHIEVE SUFFRAGE FIRST. ANTHONY ARGUED THAT "THE MOST INTELLIGENT"— REFERRING TO EDUCATED WHITE WOMEN LIKE HERSELF— BE PRIORITIZED AND SAID:

"I WILL CUT OFF THIS RIGHT ARM OF MINE BEFORE I WILL EVER WORK OR DEMAND THE BALLOT FOR THE NEGRO AND NOT THE WOMAN."

STANTON USED EVEN MORE DIRECTLY RACIST LANGUAGE, ASKING IF SHE WAS REALLY SUPPOSED TO

"STAND ASIDE AND SEE 'SAMBO' WALK INTO THE KINGDOM FIRST."

BLACK FEMINISTS KNEW, HOWEVER, THAT THE STRUGGLE WAS ONE.

"WE ARE ALL BOUND UP TOGETHER," HARPER SAID.

"IF ONE LINK OF THE CHAIN BE BROKEN, THE CHAIN IS BROKEN," ANNA JULIA HAYWOOD COOPER SAID.

GIVE WOMEN THE VOTE

BY THE TURN OF THE CENTURY, THE SUFFRAGISTS HAD A "LOOK" IN THE PUBLIC'S EYE—WHITE WOMEN, CLAD IN WHITE. BUT THE WOMEN AGITATING FOR CHANGE—BLACK, CHINESE, JEWISH, POOR, YOUNG, QUEER, DISABLED— WERE MUCH MORE DIVERSE.

OFTEN, THE MORE MARGINALIZED A WOMAN'S IDENTITY, THE MORE EXPANSIVE HER VIEW OF WHAT LIBERATION MIGHT MEAN.

BLACK SUFFRAGIST IDA B. WELLS REPORTED RELENTLESSLY ON LYNCHING, AND PUBLICLY CRITICIZED WHITE FEMINISTS WHO IGNORED THE HORRORS OF WHITE MOB VIOLENCE.

NANNIE HELEN BURROUGHS OPENED A SCHOOL TO EDUCATE AND TRAIN WORKING-CLASS BLACK WOMEN—WHO PARTICIPATED IN THE LABOR FORCE AT ALMOST FOUR TIMES THE RATE OF WHITE WOMEN— WITH CLASSES THAT RANGED FROM POWER MACHINE OPERATION TO MUSIC TO BASKETBALL.

ROSE SCHNEIDERMAN, A POLISH-JEWISH IMMIGRANT, AND SOCIALIST HELEN KELLER, WHO ROSE TO NATIONAL PROMINENCE BECAUSE OF HER DISABILITIES, RALLIED WORKING WOMEN.

VOTES FOR

SCHNEIDERMAN, WHO FAMOUSLY SAID,

"THE WORKER MUST HAVE BREAD, BUT SHE MUST HAVE ROSES, TOO," ORGANIZED TO IMPROVE WAGES, HOURS, SAFETY STANDARDS, EDUCATION, AND RECREATIONAL OPPORTUNITIES FOR WORKING WOMEN.

CHINESE AMERICAN TEEN ACTIVIST MABEL PING-HUA LEE WROTE ARTICLES AND ESSAYS IN SUPPORT OF EQUALITY AND LED A WOMEN'S SUFFRAGE PARADE ON HORSEBACK IN NEW YORK CITY AT **AGE FIFTEEN,** NEAR A LARGE BANNER THAT SAID THE SUFFRAGE MOVEMENT WAS FINALLY **"CATCHING UP WITH CHINA."**

INDIGENOUS WOMEN ALSO CONTINUED TO CHAMPION WOMEN'S RIGHTS, ALTHOUGH THE ISSUE OF AMERICAN WOMEN'S SUFFRAGE WAS CONTROVERSIAL SINCE IT WAS TIED UP WITH AMERICAN CITIZENSHIP.

FOR SOME, CITIZENSHIP WAS SEEN AS A TOOL OF ASSIMILATION. OTHERS, SUCH AS ZITKÁLA-ŠÁ, YANKTON DAKOTA SIOUX, FOUGHT FOR CITIZENSHIP RIGHTS FOR NATIVE AMERICANS, INCLUDING THE RIGHT TO VOTE.

STILL OTHERS SUCH AS ATTORNEY MARIE LOUISE BOTTINEAU BALDWIN, TURTLE MOUNTAIN OJIBWE, STARTED AS AN ASSIMILATIONIST, BUT EVOLVED HER VIEWS, BECOMING OUTSPOKEN ON HOW THE RIGHTS OF WOMEN IN NATIVE SOCIETIES **WERE SUPERIOR** TO THOSE OF AMERICAN WOMEN.

VOTES FOR

WHITE WOMEN SECURED THE VOTE IN 1920,
BUT MANY WOMEN WHO HAD BEEN
FIGHTING ALONGSIDE THEM DID NOT.

ASIAN WOMEN COULDN'T VOTE UNTIL THE IMMIGRATION AND NATIONALITY ACT
WAS PASSED IN 1952; NATIVE WOMEN COULDN'T VOTE IN EVERY STATE UNTIL 1962;
AND BLACK WOMEN WHO ATTEMPTED TO REGISTER AND VOTE IN THE 1960S WERE
HARASSED, BEATEN, AND THREATENED WITH UNEMPLOYMENT AND EVEN LYNCHING.

DURING THE 1960S AND '70S, WOMEN ACROSS
LIBERATION AND POWER MOVEMENTS—
CIVIL RIGHTS, RED POWER, CHICANO POWER, ASIAN AMERICAN, GAY—
CONTINUED TO ENVISION MORE EGALITARIAN WORLDS,
WHILE DISMANTLING SEXISM WITHIN THEIR OWN ORGANIZATIONS AND MOVEMENTS.

SEPTIMA POINSETTE CLARK,
REFERRED TO AS THE
"QUEEN MOTHER"
OF THE CIVIL RIGHTS
MOVEMENT, DEVELOPED
LITERACY AND CITIZENSHIP
WORKSHOPS. ELLA BAKER
PUSHED THE STUDENT
NONVIOLENT
COORDINATING
COMMITTEE TO
DEVELOP TWO
WINGS—

DIRECT ACTION,
AND VOTER
REGISTRATION.
FANNIE LOU HAMER
ORGANIZED THE FREEDOM
SUMMER VOTER
REGISTRATION DRIVE,
WHICH ATTEMPTED TO
REGISTER 17,000 BLACK
MISSISSIPPIANS TO VOTE.

BALLOT
BOX
25

ALL EMPOWERED ORDINARY WOMEN
TO FIGHT FOR THEMSELVES
VIA GRASSROOTS ORGANIZING.

DOLORES HUERTA, LABOR ACTIVIST AND LEADER OF THE CHICANO CIVIL RIGHTS MOVEMENT, REGISTERED MEXICAN FARMWORKERS TO VOTE, AND VIGOROUSLY FOUGHT FOR THEIR SAFETY AND HEALTHCARE.

PATSY TAKEMOTO MINK BECAME THE FIRST WOMAN OF COLOR ELECTED TO CONGRESS IN 1965, AND CHAMPIONED GREAT SOCIETY LEGISLATION, FIGHTING FOR A NATIONAL DAYCARE SYSTEM TO SUPPORT LOW-INCOME WOMEN.

AND IN 1972, SHIRLEY CHISHOLM BECAME THE FIRST WOMAN TO RUN FOR THE DEMOCRATIC PARTY'S PRESIDENTIAL NOMINATION.

IN 1974, WOMEN OF ALL RED NATIONS (WARN) WAS FOUNDED BY LORELEI DECORA MEANS, PHYLLIS YOUNG, JANET MCCLOUD, AND MADONNA THUNDER HAWK.

THE GROUP INCLUDED OVER

300 WOMEN FROM 30 NATIVE NATIONS AND ADVOCATED FOR WOMEN'S HEALTHCARE RIGHTS, CHILDREN'S RIGHTS, TREATY RIGHTS, ENVIRONMENTAL JUSTICE, AND MORE.

33

SOME WOMEN HAVE NOW HAD THE VOTE FOR OVER 100 YEARS, BUT THERE ARE STILL WOMEN FIGHTING TO BE SEEN AS WORTHY OF EQUAL RIGHTS.

TODAY'S MOST MARGINALIZED WOMEN—TRANS WOMEN, DISABLED WOMEN, UNDOCUMENTED WOMEN, INCARCERATED WOMEN—CONTINUE TO BE

DISENFRANCHISED.

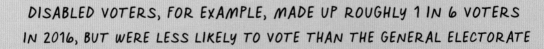

DISABLED VOTERS, FOR EXAMPLE, MADE UP ROUGHLY 1 IN 6 VOTERS IN 2016, BUT WERE LESS LIKELY TO VOTE THAN THE GENERAL ELECTORATE

DUE TO NUMEROUS BARRIERS—

POLL WORKERS UNTRAINED IN AUDIO OR LARGE-PRINT BALLOTS, A LACK OF AUTOMATIC DOOR OPENERS AND RAMPS, STATE LAWS THAT BAR PEOPLE WITH INTELLECTUAL AND COGNITIVE DISABILITIES FROM VOTING.

ALICE WONG, THE FOUNDER AND DIRECTOR OF **THE DISABILITY VISIBILITY PROJECT,** CREATED #CRIPTHEVOTE IN 2016 AS A VEHICLE FOR DISABLED PEOPLE TO BRING ATTENTION TO THE WAYS **THEIR VOTES AND VOICES ARE SUPPRESSED,** TO ADVOCATE FOR THEMSELVES, AND TO DEMAND ACCOUNTABILITY FROM ELECTED OFFICIALS.

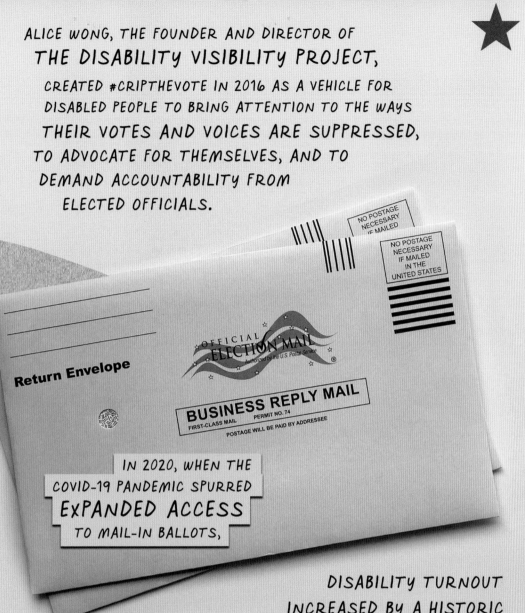

NO POSTAGE NECESSARY IF MAILED

NO POSTAGE NECESSARY IF MAILED IN THE UNITED STATES

Return Envelope

OFFICIAL ELECTION MAIL
Authorized by the U.S. Postal Service ®

BUSINESS REPLY MAIL
FIRST-CLASS MAIL   PERMIT NO. 74
POSTAGE WILL BE PAID BY ADDRESSEE

IN 2020, WHEN THE COVID-19 PANDEMIC SPURRED **EXPANDED ACCESS** TO MAIL-IN BALLOTS,

DISABILITY TURNOUT INCREASED BY A HISTORIC 6 PERCENTAGE POINTS.

REDUCING BARRIERS TO VOTING DIDN'T ONLY INCREASE THE PARTICIPATION OF DISABLED PEOPLE, IT INCREASED THE PARTICIPATION OF EVERYONE.

BECAUSE, WHEN THE MOST MARGINALIZED ARE CENTERED IN FIGHTS FOR EQUALITY, IT ONLY EXPANDS HOW WIDE THE CIRCLE FOR JUSTICE CAN BE.

A NATION OF IMMIGRANTS

"WHEN WE MELT INTO THE POT WE USUALLY
BECOME CHARRED CRUST AT THE BOTTOM."

—CHUCK D

IT WAS THE FIRST TIME AN ELECTION **WAS BROADCAST VIA RADIO,** AND THE FIRST TIME CELEBRITIES WERE BROUGHT IN TO MAKE SPEECHES, WRITE SONGS, AND OFFER ENDORSEMENTS.

IT WAS ALSO THE FIRST ELECTION IN WHICH **WHITE WOMEN COULD VOTE NATIONALLY,** AND THEY THREW THEIR SUPPORT BEHIND HARDING, NONE MORE PROMINENTLY THAN FAMED SINGER/ACTRESS AND OUTSPOKEN SUFFRAGIST **LILLIAN RUSSELL,** WHO MADE THREE OR FOUR SPEECHES A DAY ON HARDING'S BEHALF ACROSS FIFTEEN STATES FOR WEEKS.

THE EFFORTS PAID OFF. HARDING WON.

ONCE ELECTED, HARDING MADE IMMIGRATION A PRIORITY.

RESTRICTIONIST IMMIGRATION EFFORTS HAD BEEN BUILDING FOR YEARS—
THE CHINESE EXCLUSION ACT WAS PASSED IN 1882, AND THE IMMIGRATION ACT OF 1917
CREATED AN EVEN WIDER ASIATIC BARRED ZONE AND

BLOCKED THE IMMIGRATION OF "UNDESIRABLE" PEOPLE

(A BROAD LIST THAT INCLUDED ALCOHOLICS, ANARCHISTS, "IDIOTS,"
"INSANE PERSONS," OPENLY QUEER PEOPLE, "PHYSICALLY DEFECTIVE"
PEOPLE, AND MANY OTHERS).

HARDING WANTED TO GO FURTHER. JUST TWO MONTHS AFTER HE WAS
SWORN IN, HE CALLED ON CONGRESS TO PASS THE EMERGENCY QUOTA ACT,
WHICH CAPPED VISAS FOR NEW IMMIGRANTS AND
CREATED A QUOTA SYSTEM THAT LIMITED ENTRY
BY COUNTRY OF ORIGIN.

THE FOLLLOWING YEAR, HE APPOINTED AN IMMIGRATION INSPECTOR
TO GO TO EUROPE ON A FACT-FINDING MISSION TO INFORM FURTHER
MEASURES. RATHER THAN SEND AN EXPERT, HE SENT HIS
CELEBRITY SUPPORTER LILLIAN RUSSELL,
WHO TOLD THE PRESS SHE WAS

"GREATLY INTERESTED IN IMMIGRATION PROBLEMS"

AND WAS GOING TO FIND OUT

"WHY THE PASSPORTS OF DELINQUENTS WERE [GIVEN VISAS] AT ALL."

CENTRAL NEWS PHOTO SERVICE, NEW YORK.

NEW YORK CITY

49

LILLIAN RUSSELL SAILS AS SPECIAL IMMIGRATION
INSPECTOR
Russell and her husband, Alexander P. Moore, publisher of
aboard the S. S. George Wash-

RUSSELL WARNED THAT EUROPE WAS READY TO RELEASE

"THOUSANDS OF IMMIGRANTS, MOST OF THEM UNDESIRABLE...

LOWER EAST SIDE DENIZENS."

IN RESPONSE, SHE PROPOSED AN IMMIGRATION FREEZE
FOR FIVE YEARS; A LAW THAT REQUIRED IMMIGRANTS TO LIVE
IN THE U.S. FOR TWENTY-ONE YEARS BEFORE BEING PERMITTED TO VOTE;
AND FOR IMMIGRATION OFFICIALS TO "SIFT" IMMIGRANTS
ABROAD VIA RIGID PHYSICAL AND MENTAL TESTS.

"WE TAKE IN TOO FEW PRODUCTIVE IMMIGRANTS AND TOO MANY DESTRUCTIVE,"
SHE SAID.

"THE MELTING POT HAS BEEN OVERCROWDED. IT HAS BOILED TOO QUICKLY AND IS RUNNING OVER,"
SHE SAID.

"WE HAVE OPENED OUR NATIONAL GATES TO HUMAN BEINGS DESIRING TO SETTLE AMONG US WITHOUT MUCH RESTRICTION AS TO MORAL CONSIDERATION OR PURITY OF BLOOD,"
SHE SAID.

"IF WE DON'T KEEP UP THE BARS, AND MAKE THEM HIGHER AND STRONGER, THERE WILL NO LONGER BE AN

AMERICA
FOR
AMERICANS,"
SHE SAID.

ANOTHER HOUSE IMMIGRATION COMMITTEE "EXPERT," PROMINENT EUGENICIST HARRY LAUGHLIN, ECHOED RUSSELL'S TESTIMONY TO CONGRESS, ARGUING FOR TIGHTER RESTRICTIONS, TO KEEP OUT

"DEFECTIVE, DEPENDENT, AND DELINQUENT CLASSES."

THE HOUSE COMMITTEE WAS SWAYED, AND THE EMERGENCY QUOTA ACT WAS RENEWED FOR ANOTHER TWO YEARS.

BY THE TIME IT EXPIRED, QUOTAS WERE NORMALIZED, AND RESTRICTIONISTS DECIDED TO PUSH FOR SOMETHING ENDURING.

CONGRESS PASSED THE JOHNSON-REED ACT OVERWHELMINGLY IN 1924.

THE ACT OPENLY SOUGHT TO PRESERVE A PREDOMINANTLY WHITE, NORTHERN, AND WESTERN EUROPEAN RACIAL MAKEUP OF THE COUNTRY BY DRAMATICALLY REDUCING IMMIGRATION FROM EVERYWHERE ELSE.

IT USED THE 1890 CENSUS AS A BASELINE—
A TIME BEFORE THE WAVES OF IMMIGRANTS FROM
SOUTHERN AND EASTERN EUROPE ARRIVED—
AND EXPANDED THE ASIATIC BARRED ZONE.

IT ALSO PROVIDED AMPLE FUNDING FOR
DEPORTATION COURTS AND
FORMED THE U.S. BORDER PATROL.

"THE RACIAL COMPOSITION OF AMERICA
AT THE PRESENT TIME THUS IS
MADE PERMANENT,"
SENATOR REED TRIUMPHED.

IMMIGRATION PLUMMETED
BY 97 PERCENT.

THE ACT HAD POWERFUL CONSEQUENCES BEYOND JUST
HALTING IMMIGRATION. IT WAS THE ACT ADOLF HITLER
REPEATEDLY REFERENCED AS A SUCCESSFUL MODEL OF
RACIAL EXCLUSION,
AND THE ACT THAT BARRED MILLIONS OF JEWISH PEOPLE
FROM SEEKING REFUGE IN THE U.S. WHEN
HIS HORRIFIC VISION CAME TO PASS.

ONE OF THE DISSENTING VOTES AGAINST THE JOHNSON-REED ACT WAS A YOUNG, FIRST-TERM GERMAN JEWISH REPRESENTATIVE FROM BROOKLYN, EMANUEL CELLER.

THE ACT HORRIFIED HIM,

AND HE SPENT THE NEXT FORTY YEARS OF HIS CAREER TRYING TO OVERTURN IT.

IN 1965, HE FINALLY SUCCEEDED.

THE HART-CELLER ACT REPLACED THE NATIONAL ORIGINS QUOTA FOR A SEVEN-CATEGORY PREFERENCE SYSTEM THAT PRIORITIZED FAMILY REUNIFICATION, SKILLED WORKERS, AND REFUGEES, WHICH IS VERY SIMILAR TO THE IMMIGRATION PROCESS AND LAWS IN PLACE TODAY.

AROUND THE SAME TIME, THE AMERICAN STORY AROUND IMMIGRATION SHIFTED.

THE IDEA OF AMERICA AS A "MELTING POT" WHERE DIFFERENT ETHNICITIES FROM ALL AROUND THE WORLD FUSE TOGETHER BEGAN TO BE SEEN AS SOMETHING POSITIVE, THE MOLTEN CORE OF THE AMERICAN DREAM.

SINCE THE ACT WAS PASSED, IMMIGRATION HAS MORE THAN

QUADRUPLED—

ESPECIALLY FROM LATIN AMERICA AND ASIA. AND ALTHOUGH THE STORY OF MODERN AMERICA AS A NATION OF IMMIGRANTS HAS BECAME A POINT OF NATIONAL PRIDE IN THEORY, IN PRACTICE IMMIGRATION HAS

BECOME INCREASINGLY CRIMINALIZED SINCE THE EARLY 1980S.

WHILE RONALD REAGAN KICKED IT OFF, EVERY PRESIDENT SINCE—NO MATTER THE POLITICAL PARTY—HAS ENGAGED IN INCREASING ANTI-IMMIGRANT ENFORCEMENT.

THE MEXICAN-U.S. BORDER HAS BECOME

EVER MORE MILITARIZED

SINCE THE MID-1990S, THE BUDGET FOR IMMIGRATION DETENTION HAS CLIMBED STEADILY UPWARD, AND DEPORTATIONS HAVE SKYROCKETED.

BARACK OBAMA'S AGGRESSIVE DEPORTATION TACTICS EARNED HIM THE NICKNAME

"DEPORTER IN CHIEF,"

AND DONALD TRUMP RODE INTO OFFICE WITH SUPPORTERS CHANTING SLOGANS THAT ECHOED LILLIAN RUSSELL'S REPORT—

"MAKE AMERICA GREAT AGAIN."

"BUILD THE WALL."

ain
he e

he analysi
it appears
e is a simple
, and is, in n
ited. The typical
a dominant trait ar

TRADITIONAL FAMILY VALUES

"THEY TOOK OUR PAST WITH A SWORD AND OUR LAND WITH A PEN. NOW THEY'RE TRYING TO TAKE OUR FUTURE WITH A SCALPEL."

—*AKWESASNE NOTES*, A NEWSPAPER PUBLISHED BY THE MOHAWK NATION

FITTER FAMILIES FOR FUTURE FIRESIDES

FITTER FAMILIES FOR FUTURE FIRESIDES

FITTER BABIES

The Eugenics Building At the Kansas Free Fair, Topeka. Prizes for Best Families and Individuals.

THE KANSAS FREE

6 BIG NIGHTS

6 BIG DAYS

THE GATES STAND OPEN

BY 1920, THE KANSAS

FREE FAIR

HAD GROWN INTO A
MASSIVE, SPRAWLING EVENT.

HUNDREDS OF THOUSANDS OF VISITORS TREKKED IN TO
WANDER ROWS UPON ROWS OF TENTS, PAVILIONS,
AND DISPLAYS THAT SHOWCASED EVERYTHING FROM
FARM MACHINERY TO WASHING MACHINES,
GOOD ROADS TO PLUMBING FIXTURES.

THERE WERE PIGS, GOATS, CHICKENS, CAR RACES,
HORSE RACES, FERRIS WHEELS, FOOD, PARADES, BANDS,
AND PRIZES
AWARDED FOR EVERYTHING FROM
BEST BULLS TO BEST CAKES TO
BEST FAMILIES.

MOVE TO IMPROVE
BEST KANSAS CROP

"Fitter Families for Future
Firesides"

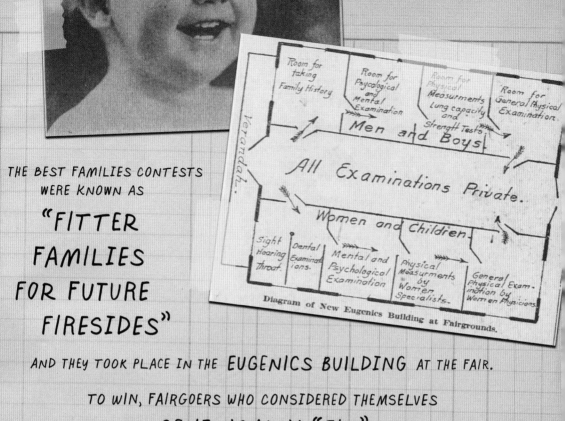

Diagram of New Eugenics Building at Fairgrounds.

THE BEST FAMILIES CONTESTS WERE KNOWN AS

"FITTER FAMILIES FOR FUTURE FIRESIDES"

AND THEY TOOK PLACE IN THE EUGENICS BUILDING AT THE FAIR.

TO WIN, FAIRGOERS WHO CONSIDERED THEMSELVES

GENETICALLY "FIT"

SIGNED UP TO UNDERGO A THREE-HOUR EXAMINATION THAT ASSESSED THEM ON EVERYTHING FROM THEIR MEDICAL HISTORY TO THEIR IQ TO THEIR PERSONALITY AND TEMPERAMENT.

THE WINNERS (WHO WERE NEARLY ALL WHITE, PROTESTANT, ABLE-BODIED, EDUCATED, AND RURAL) WERE BRANDED

"GRADE A" HUMAN STOCK.

BON BONS, FEW CLOTHES HARMFUL, SAYS "FITTEST FAMILY" MOTHER

WHILE FAIRGOERS WAITED TO BE EXAMINED,
THEY WERE SHOWN INFORMATIONAL DISPLAYS
THAT TALKED ABOUT THE IMPORTANCE OF
"EUGENIC MARRIAGES" THAT COULD
"BREED OUT" UNWANTED CHARACTERISTICS
LIKE PHYSICAL AND MENTAL DISABILITIES, CRIMINALITY,
AND POVERTY IN ORDER TO PRODUCE DESIRABLE

"PURE" CHILDREN.

THE AMERICAN EUGENICS MOVEMENT WAS MAINSTREAM AT THE TIME (THEODORE
ROOSEVELT, ALEXANDER GRAHAM BELL, AND JOHN D. ROCKEFELLER JR.
WERE OUTSPOKEN SUPPORTERS AND OTHERS LIKE HELEN KELLER WERE
BRIEFLY SWAYED), AND FOR FARM FAMILIES ACCUSTOMED TO
BREEDING PRIZEWINNING JERSEY COWS AND SWEETER
CORN, THE APPROACH SOUNDED SCIENTIFIC, AND
SEEMED TO MAKE A LOT OF SENSE.

WHILE FAIR FAMILIES WHO
DIDN'T WIN GRADE A STATUS
WERE TYPICALLY GIVEN
BENIGN TREATMENTS
(LIKE THE ADVICE TO
DRINK MORE MILK),
OTHER INDIVIDUALS
SOCIETY HAD DEEMED

GENETICALLY
"UNFIT,"

LIKE THOSE IN STATE-RUN
INSTITUTIONS
AND PRISONS,
WERE TREATED IN A
MUCH MORE
SEVERE
WAY.

TO STOP THOSE INDIVIDUALS FROM PASSING ON THEIR GENES,
DOCTORS ROUTINELY PERFORMED COMPULSORY STERILIZATIONS—
THE PRACTICE OF FORCIBLY REMOVING THE ABILITY OF CERTAIN PEOPLE
TO HAVE CHILDREN—IN STATES ACROSS THE COUNTRY THROUGHOUT
THE EARLY 20TH CENTURY.

IT'S ESTIMATED THAT BY 1963,

64,000 AMERICANS

HAD BEEN FORCIBLY STERILIZED,
20,000 IN CALIFORNIA ALONE.

THE AMERICAN EUGENICS MOVEMENT FELL
OUT OF FAVOR AFTER AMERICANS
WITNESSED HITLER'S HORRIFIC
APPLICATION OF EUGENIC THEORY
DURING WORLD WAR II.

BUT THE UNDERLYING IDEA
THAT SOME PEOPLE ARE

GOOD FOR
SOCIETY

WHILE OTHERS ARE A
BURDEN
REMAINED.

TALK SHIFTED FROM UNFIT GENES TO UNFIT MOTHERS.

WHILE BEFORE WORLD WAR II, STERILIZATION EFFORTS FOCUSED ON THE INSTITUTIONALIZED AND IMPRISONED, AFTER THE WAR MARGINALIZED PEOPLE OUTSIDE INSTITUTIONS—ESPECIALLY POOR, BLACK, NATIVE, AND HISPANIC WOMEN— **BECAME THE TARGETS.**

SOCIAL WORKERS STEERED THESE WOMEN TOWARD STERILIZATION BY THREATENING TO TAKE AWAY THEIR SOCIAL WELFARE BENEFITS, **OR THEIR CHILDREN,** IF THEY DIDN'T AGREE TO THE PROCEDURE.

DOCTORS MISINFORMED WOMEN ABOUT THE PROCEDURES, IMPLYING THAT THEY WERE REVERSIBLE OR NEGLECTING TO INFORM THEM ABOUT OTHER, SAFER, NONPERMANENT FORMS OF BIRTH CONTROL.

NURSES GAVE WOMEN CONFUSING FORMS IN A LANGUAGE THEY MIGHT NOT SPEAK. DOCTORS WITHHELD PAINKILLERS FROM WOMEN DURING CHILDBIRTH, REFUSING TO DELIVER BABIES IF STERILIZATION CONSENT FORMS WEREN'T SIGNED. IN SOME CASES, DOCTORS ASKED FOR CONSENT **THE DAY AFTER THE PROCEDURE.**

WOMEN SPOKE OUT.

FANNIE LOU HAMER, A CIVIL RIGHTS LEADER, ACTIVIST, AND ORGANIZER, GAVE A SPEECH ABOUT THE PREVALENCE OF STERILIZATION AMONG POOR BLACK WOMEN IN MISSISSIPPI, A PRACTICE SO COMMON IT WAS KNOWN AS A "MISSISSIPPI APPENDECTOMY."

"SIX OUT OF EVERY TEN NEGRO WOMEN WERE TAKEN TO THE SUNFLOWER CITY HOSPITAL TO BE STERILIZED FOR NO REASON AT ALL," SHE SAID.

SHE KNEW, BECAUSE SHE WAS ONE OF THEM.

IN THE EARLY 1970S,
ANTONIA HERNÁNDEZ, A YOUNG LAWYER,
WAS TIPPED OFF BY A MEDICAL RESIDENT,
DR. BERNARD ROSENFELD, ABOUT ROUTINE,
COERCED STERILIZATIONS OF SPANISH-SPEAKING,
WORKING-CLASS WOMEN AT LOS ANGELES
COUNTY HOSPITAL.

SHE FOUND THE WOMEN AND ENCOURAGED A GROUP OF
THEM TO FILE SUIT AGAINST THE HOSPITAL IN 1975.

DR. HELEN RODRÍGUEZ TRÍAS HELPED FOUND THE
COMMITTEE TO END STERILIZATION ABUSE IN 1970
AFTER SEEING HOW COMMON THE PROCEDURES
WERE IN PUERTO RICO—BY 1965,
TWO OUT OF THREE PUERTO RICAN
WOMEN IN THEIR EARLY TWENTIES
HAD BEEN STERILIZED.

DR. CONSTANCE REDBIRD PINKERTON-URI, A CHEROKEE-CHOCTAW PHYSICIAN, BEGAN INTERVIEWING NATIVE WOMEN ABOUT THEIR EXPERIENCES WITH INDIAN HEALTH SERVICE (THE U.S. GOVERNMENT HEALTHCARE PROVIDED TO TRIBAL NATIONS) AFTER A WOMAN CAME TO HER LOOKING FOR A "WOMB TRANSPLANT," NOT KNOWING HER STERILIZATION WAS PERMANENT.

IN INTERVIEWS SHE FOUND THAT THE STERILIZATIONS WERE OFTEN GIVEN WITHOUT INFORMED CONSENT, FOR RIDICULOUS REASONS, AND UNDER DURESS. ONE WOMAN WENT TO A DOCTOR COMPLAINING OF HEADACHES AND WAS PRESCRIBED STERILIZATION (SHE HAD A BRAIN TUMOR).

OTHERS WERE TOLD THEIR CHILDREN WOULD BE TAKEN AWAY IF THEY DIDN'T COMPLY—AN OMINOUS THREAT WHEN ONE IN THREE NATIVE CHILDREN WERE BEING FORCIBLY PLACED IN FOSTER CARE IN THE 1970S, AND U.S.-RUN INDIAN BOARDING SCHOOLS HAD BEEN WRENCHING NATIVE CHILDREN FROM THEIR FAMILIES FOR A CENTURY—AN ACT OF GENOCIDE UNTO ITSELF.

IT'S ESTIMATED THAT ONE QUARTER TO ONE HALF OF ALL NATIVE WOMEN WERE STERILIZED IN THE 1970S.

OVERALL, BETWEEN

100,000 AND 150,000

LOW-INCOME WOMEN WERE STERILIZED
UNDER FEDERAL PROGRAMS IN THE
LATE 1960S AND EARLY 1970S.

BECAUSE OF THE WOMEN WHO
SPOKE OUT,

AND THE ACTIVISTS WHO FOUGHT
ALONGSIDE THEM,

BY THE EARLY 1980S, LAWS AND PRACTICES
AROUND INFORMED CONSENT CHANGED, AND
WIDESPREAD COERCED STERILIZATIONS STOPPED.

BUT THEY DIDN'T STOP
FOR EVERYONE.

THE NOTION THAT SOME HUMANS
SHOULD NOT PASS ON THEIR
GENES PERSISTS.

INCARCERATED WOMEN, INTERSEX
CHILDREN, WOMEN IN IMMIGRANT DETENTION
CENTERS—NUMEROUS CASES OF DOCUMENTED
COERCED STERILIZATION WERE BROUGHT TO LIGHT FROM 2006-2020.

AND, TO THIS DAY, DISABLED PEOPLE ARE STILL FIGHTING
FOR THE RIGHT TO MAKE DECISIONS ABOUT THEIR OWN BODIES
AND LIVES, INCLUDING THE RIGHT TO BE FREE FROM INVOLUNTARY
STERILIZATIONS PERFORMED "FOR THEIR OWN GOOD."

ONE NATION UNDER GOD

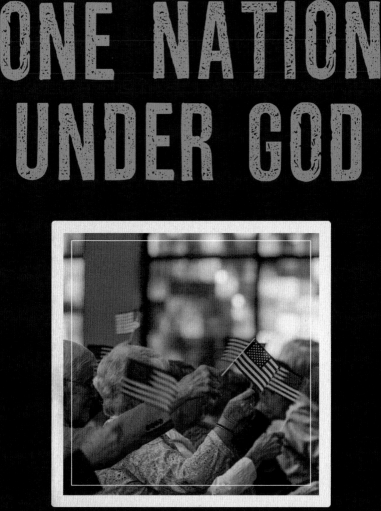

"THIS IS THE ULTIMATE TRAGEDY OF SEGREGATION.
IT NOT ONLY HARMS ONE PHYSICALLY,
BUT IT INJURES ONE SPIRITUALLY."

IN 1976, AMERICA WAS FLOODED WITH **PATRIOTIC PROGRAMMING AND COLLECTIBLES** IN HONOR OF THE NATION'S **200TH ANNIVERSARY.**

JERRY FALWELL, A BAPTIST PASTOR WHO REGULARLY PREACHED TO **15 MILLION** PEOPLE VIA HIS NATIONALLY SYNDICATED TELEVISION MINISTRY, **THE OLD-TIME GOSPEL HOUR,** SEIZED ON THE MOMENT BY HOSTING **"I LOVE AMERICA"** RALLIES IN OVER 100 CITIES ACROSS THE COUNTRY.

COVERAGE OF THE RALLIES
IN NEWSPAPERS FROM COLORADO
SPRINGS TO GREEN BAY CALLED THEM AN
"INSPIRATIONAL MUSICAL-DRAMATIC PROGRAM"
THAT INCLUDED SCENES OF
"WASHINGTON PRAYING AT VALLEY FORGE, MARINES
RAISING THE FLAG ON IWO JIMA AND AMERICAN ASTRONAUTS
PLACING THE 'STARS AND STRIPES' ON THE SURFACE OF THE MOON."

THE PRODUCTION INCLUDED AN ORCHESTRA, SEVENTY-FIVE RED-, WHITE-, AND
BLUE-CLAD STUDENT SINGERS FROM FALWELL'S LIBERTY BAPTIST COLLEGE,
LOTS AND LOTS OF AMERICAN FLAGS,
AND FALWELL HIMSELF, WHO PREACHED THAT AMERICA HAD TURNED AWAY
FROM GOD AND NEEDED TO RETURN TO THE FAITH OF THE FOUNDING FATHERS.

THE MASH-UP OF GOSPEL MUSIC AND PATRIOTIC SONGS INTENTIONALLY
BLURRED THE LINE BETWEEN GOD AND GOVERNMENT,
AND FALWELL URGED PIOUS AUDIENCE MEMBERS
TO BE MORE POLITICALLY ACTIVE.

AT HIS JULY 4TH BICENTENNIAL RALLY, HE SAID "THIS IDEA OF
'RELIGION AND POLITICS DON'T MIX' WAS INVENTED BY THE DEVIL
TO KEEP CHRISTIANS FROM RUNNING THEIR OWN COUNTRY."

1976 WAS ALSO AN ELECTION YEAR.

BOTH PRESIDENTIAL CANDIDATES—GERALD FORD AND JIMMY CARTER—DEFINED THEMSELVES AS **BORN-AGAIN CHRISTIANS,** ALTHOUGH CARTER WAS THE ONLY ONE WHO PUT HIS FAITH FRONT AND CENTER ON THE CAMPAIGN TRAIL.

THE ENSUING NATIONAL MEDIA ATTENTION PUSHED EVANGELICAL CHRISTIANITY FROM THE **MARGINS TO THE MAINSTREAM,** CAUSING NEWSWEEK TO DUB 1976 AS "THE YEAR OF THE **EVANGELICALS.**"

CARTER'S FAITH RESONATED STRONGLY WITH FELLOW AMERICAN EVANGELICALS—AN ESTIMATED **50 MILLION PEOPLE, WHO CLAIMED TO BE "BORN AGAIN,"** ABOUT HALF OF WHOM WERE FUNDAMENTALISTS, PEOPLE WHO TEND TO READ THE BIBLE LITERALLY.

BUT AT THE TIME, MANY EVANGELICALS WEREN'T REGISTERED TO VOTE.

THOSE WHO WERE DIDN'T VOTE AS A BLOC—NOT EVEN ALL FUNDAMENTALISTS WERE CONSISTENTLY CONSERVATIVE ON SOCIAL AND POLITICAL ISSUES.

CARTER WON THE ELECTION, BUT A FEW YEARS INTO HIS PRESIDENCY, MANY EVANGELICALS WERE **DISAPPOINTED WITH HIS POLICIES.**

CARTER PERSONALLY OPPOSED ABORTION AND DIDN'T PUBLICLY SUPPORT THE 1973 ROE V. WADE RULING THAT LEGALIZED IT, BUT HE ALSO APPOINTED **JUDGES WHO WERE SUPPORTIVE OF ROE,** AND HE DIDN'T SEEK A CONSTITUTIONAL AMENDMENT TO OUTLAW IT. HE AGREED WITH THE SUPREME COURT THAT OFFICIAL **SCHOOL PRAYER** WAS A VIOLATION OF THE FIRST AMENDMENT, HE SIGNED THE CIVIL SERVICE REFORM ACT, **WHICH PROTECTED LGBTQ WORKERS,** AND HE SUPPORTED THE EQUAL RIGHTS AMENDMENT WHICH SOUGHT TO GUARANTEE **LEGAL GENDER EQUALITY.**

CONSERVATIVE PREACHERS LIKE FALWELL BALKED, AND CITED RISING DIVORCE RATES, RISING ABORTION RATES, SCHOOLS TEACHING "PORNOGRAPHY" (I.E., SEX ED), AND GAY PEOPLE BECOMING GRADUALLY MORE ACCEPTED AS EVIDENCE OF A COUNTRY IN

MORAL FREE FALL.

FALWELL AND OTHER CONSERVATIVE CHRISTIANS
WANTED CARTER OUT.

FALWELL'S INCREASING FOCUS ON POLITICS CAUGHT
THE EYE OF PAUL WEYRICH, A CONSERVATIVE POLITICAL
ACTIVIST AND FOUNDER OF THE HERITAGE FOUNDATION,
A THINK TANK FOCUSED ON PROMOTING
CONSERVATIVE PUBLIC POLICIES.

WEYRICH HAD BEEN TRYING TO FIND A WAY TO
GALVANIZE EVANGELICALS INTO AN
INFLUENTIAL CONSERVATIVE VOTING BLOC
FOR YEARS, BUT HAD FAILED TO FIND AN ISSUE THAT
OUTRAGED THEM ENOUGH TO MAKE THEM ACT.

HE TRIED **ABORTION,**

HE TRIED **WOMEN'S RIGHTS,**

HE TRIED **PORNOGRAPHY,**

BUT NOTHING SPURRED ACTION
FROM EVANGELICAL LEADERS.

NOTHING UNTIL THE IRS STARTED
GOING AFTER THE TAX-EXEMPT STATUS OF
RACIALLY SEGREGATED SCHOOLS.

FOLLOWING THE SUPREME COURT DECISION BROWN V.
BOARD OF ED IN 1954, WHICH RULED THAT RACIAL SEGREGATION
IN PUBLIC SCHOOLS WAS UNCONSTITUTIONAL,
WAVES OF WHITE STUDENTS BEGAN
TO FLEE PUBLIC SCHOOLS TO AVOID
INTEGRATION IN THE 1960S.

PRIVATE, WHITES-ONLY CHRISTIAN ACADEMIES OPENED TO TAKE THEM IN.

FALWELL—WHO WAS AN ARDENT SEGREGATIONIST, RAILED AGAINST "LEFT-WING" DR. MARTIN LUTHER KING JR., AND CALLED THE 1964 CIVIL RIGHTS ACT "CIVIL WRONGS"—FOUNDED HIS OWN PRIVATE, WHITES-ONLY SCHOOL, LYNCHBURG CHRISTIAN ACADEMY, IN 1966.

SINCE THE SCHOOLS WEREN'T FEDERALLY FUNDED, THEIR ADMINISTRATORS DIDN'T THINK THEY HAD TO ABIDE BY MANDATORY INTEGRATION. BUT AS RELIGIOUS SCHOOLS THEY WERE CONSIDERED **"CHARITABLE INSTITUTIONS,"** AND THEREFORE TAX-EXEMPT.

WHEN THE SUPREME COURT RULED IN 1971 THAT SEGREGATED SCHOOLS COULD NO LONGER BE **CONSIDERED CHARITABLE INSTITUTIONS,** THE IRS BEGAN WARNING CHRISTIAN ACADEMIES THAT THEIR TAX-EXEMPT STATUS WOULD BE **REVOKED, AND THAT THEY'D OWE BACK TAXES, IF THEY REMAINED SEGREGATED.**

SOME, LIKE LYNCHBURG CHRISTIAN ACADEMY, BROKE DOWN WITHIN A FEW YEARS AND CHANGED THEIR ADMISSIONS POLICIES. OTHERS, LIKE BOB JONES UNIVERSITY, REFUSED TO INTEGRATE FOR YEARS, **AND IN 1976, ITS TAX-EXEMPT STATUS WAS REVOKED.**

EVANGELICALS THOUGHT THE FEDERAL GOVERNMENT HAD NO BUSINESS TELLING THEM HOW TO RAISE THEIR CHILDREN, AND THEY WERE READY TO **MAKE THEIR VOICES HEARD.**

WEYRICH AND FALWELL FOUNDED

THE MORAL MAJORITY—

A LOBBYING GROUP, POLITICAL ACTION COMMITTEE, LEGAL FUND, AND EDUCATIONAL OUTREACH GROUP— TO MOBILIZE CONSERVATIVE VOTERS IN 1979.

WHILE THEY KNEW PRO-SEGREGATION WAS THE ISSUE THAT DROVE THEIR VOTERS, THEY WERE SAVVY ENOUGH TO REALIZE IT **WASN'T POLITICALLY PALATABLE.**

SO, THEY DEVELOPED

"PRO-FAMILY"

MESSAGING INSTEAD.

PRO-FAMILY SOUNDED A LOT BETTER THAN PRO-SEGREGATION, AND IT WAS VAGUE ENOUGH AND BROAD ENOUGH TO ENCOMPASS ALL THE ISSUES THEY WANTED TO HAMMER ON— ANTI-ABORTION RIGHTS, ANTI-GAY RIGHTS, ANTI-WOMEN'S EQUALITY, ANTI-INTEGRATION.

IT ALSO IMPLIED THAT IF SOMEONE WAS FOR ANY OF THOSE ISSUES, THEY WERE ANTI-FAMILY.

Let Me Know Where You Stand On These Burning Issues:

Do you approve of the present laws legalizing ABORTION-ON-DEMAND?

☐ YES   ☐ NO

Do you approve of PORNOGRAPHIC and obscene classroom textbooks being used under the guise of sex education?

☐ YES   ☐ NO

Do you approve of the American flag being burned in liberal and radical ANTI-AMERICAN DEMONSTRATIONS?

☐ YES   ☐ NO

Do you approve of the ratification of the ERA which could well lead to HOMOSEXUAL MARRIAGES, unisexual bathrooms, and, of course, the mandatory drafting of women for military combat?

☐ YES   ☐ NO

HE REPORTED THAT HUNDREDS OF THOUSANDS VOTED,
AND THAT 95.8 PERCENT OF ALL AMERICANS
WERE ON THE SIDE OF BIBLE MORALITY.

HENCE, THE MORAL MAJORITY.

WITH THE 1980 ELECTION COMING UP, THE MORAL MAJORITY FOCUSED ON ENERGIZING CONSERVATIVE CHRISTIAN VOTERS, AND IT HAD THE VEHICLE TO DO IT—

CHRISTIAN
MEDIA

HAD BALLOONED DURING THE 1970S. BY 1980, THERE WERE THIRTY CHRISTIAN-ORIENTED TV STATIONS, MORE THAN ONE THOUSAND CHRISTIAN RADIO STATIONS, AND FOUR CHRISTIAN NETWORKS, AND MOST WERE CONTROLLED BY

RIGHT-WING FUNDAMENTALIST GROUPS.

FALWELL REPRISED HIS "I LOVE AMERICA" RALLIES, WHICH BECAME EVEN MORE OVERTLY POLITICAL, TAKING PLACE ON STATE CAPITOLS ACROSS THE COUNTRY, AND INCLUDING CONSERVATIVE POLITICIANS WHO SOUGHT FALWELL'S TACIT ENDORSEMENT.

FALWELL WAS INCREDIBLY SUCCESSFUL AT FUNDRAISING NOT JUST THROUGH RALLIES, BUT THROUGH HIS TELEVISION MINISTRY AND "I LOVE AMERICA CLUB."

IN 1979, HE RAISED $35 MILLION FROM THE 2.5 MILLION PEOPLE ON THE OLD-TIME GOSPEL HOUR'S MAILING LIST.

Huge Rally Mixes God, Government

Falwell rally mixes religion, politics
Sun shines warmly on television evangelist's Capitol extravaganza

God, country, and old-time gospel

HIS MAILING LISTS ALSO GOT
MORE SOPHISTICATED.
WITH NEW COMPUTERIZED DIRECT
MAIL TECHNIQUES, LISTS COULD BE
SEGMENTED, AND MESSAGING COULD
BE HONED DEPENDING ON WHO
FALWELL WANTED TO
ENGAGE (AND ENRAGE).

MOST CRITICALLY,
THE MORAL MAJORITY ORGANIZED
A MASSIVE VOTER
REGISTRATION DRIVE,

REGISTERING OVER 4 MILLION
NEW VOTERS IN 1980 ALONE.
RONALD REAGAN WASN'T CONSERVATIVES' IDEAL
CANDIDATE (HE WAS LESS RELIGIOUS THAN CARTER,
TWICE-MARRIED, AND HAD SIGNED A PERMISSIVE
ABORTION BILL AS GOVERNOR OF CALIFORNIA), BUT HE
WAS THE MORE CONSERVATIVE CANDIDATE, AND HE
PROMISED TO APPOINT ANTI-ABORTION JUDGES AND
FIX THE TAX ISSUE FOR CHRISTIAN SCHOOLS.

ONE-FIFTH
OF THE MORAL MAJORITY VOTERS
WHO VOTED FOR CARTER
SWITCHED TO REAGAN
IN 1980, AND REAGAN ENDED UP
WINNING THE ELECTION
BY A LANDSLIDE.

REAGAN

FALWELL AND
THE MORAL MAJORITY
HAPPILY TOOK
THE CREDIT.

ALTHOUGH REAGAN DIDN'T PULL OFF MANY OF THE POLICY CHANGES THE MORAL MAJORITY SOUGHT, **THE WHITE EVANGELICAL CONSERVATIVE VOTING BLOC** WAS SECURELY ESTABLISHED, AND IT BECAME AN **INCREASINGLY POWERFUL POLITICAL FORCE** IN SUBSEQUENT ELECTIONS, THROWING ITS SUPPORT BEHIND GEORGE W. BUSH, JOHN MCCAIN, AND MITT ROMNEY.

FORTY YEARS AFTER THE BICENTENNIAL, ANOTHER FALWELL, JERRY FALWELL JR., WAS ON THE CAMPAIGN TRAIL, RALLYING CONSERVATIVE EVANGELICAL VOTERS TO THE POLLS. AGAIN, THE CANDIDATE WAS A DIVORCED CELEBRITY WHO WAS NOT KNOWN FOR HIS RELIGIOUS CONVICTION AND WHO HAD BEEN PRO-CHOICE IN THE PAST.

STILL, 80 PERCENT OF WHITE EVANGELICALS VOTED FOR DONALD TRUMP. AND THEY STUCK WITH HIM THROUGHOUT HIS TEMPESTUOUS ADMINISTRATION, WITH 76 PERCENT VOTING FOR HIM AGAIN IN 2020.

"I THINK HE'S GOING TO END UP BEING OUR GREATEST PRESIDENT SINCE GEORGE WASHINGTON," FALWELL JR. SAID.

81

HOME OF THE BRAVE

"ONCE THERE WAS A TERRIBLE DISEASE IN THIS COUNTRY AND ALL OVER THE WORLD, AND . . . A BRAVE GROUP OF PEOPLE STOOD UP AND FOUGHT AND, IN SOME CASES, GAVE THEIR LIVES SO THAT OTHER PEOPLE MIGHT LIVE AND BE FREE."

— VITO RUSSO

IN JULY OF 1983, THE MORAL MAJORITY'S MONTHLY NEWSPAPER,

THE MORAL MAJORITY REPORT,

WAS FULL OF ITS USUAL FARE—
THE LATEST ABOUT BOB JONES, THE LATEST ABOUT ABORTION,
A FULL-PAGE AD FOR A JULY 4TH "I LOVE AMERICA" RALLY.

IT ALSO FEATURED ITS FIRST COVER STORY
ABOUT THE BURGEONING AIDS CRISIS.

AIDS

—A BLACK BAR BOLDLY PROCLAIMED ABOVE A PICTURE OF
A WHITE MOM, DAD, AND THEIR TWO YOUNG KIDS
WITH WORRIED EYES AND WEARING SURGICAL MASKS—

"HOMOSEXUAL DISEASES THREATEN AMERICAN FAMILIES."

THE STORY WENT ON TO RAIL AGAINST A "GAY PLAGUE" BEING
SPREAD "INSIDE AND OUTSIDE THE GAY GHETTOS OF AMERICA" BY A
"MALIGNANT MINORITY" THREATENING "DEFENSELESS HETEROSEXUALS."

1983 WAS STILL THE EARLY DAYS OF THE AIDS EPIDEMIC—
(RONALD REAGAN FAMOUSLY DIDN'T UTTER
THE WORD "AIDS" FOR ANOTHER TWO YEARS),
BUT THE MORAL MAJORITY WAS ALREADY REPORTING THAT

FEARS ABOUT "CATCHING" AIDS

WERE GROWING SHARPLY, WITH "WORRIED CITIZENS" CALLING
HOTLINES TO SEE IF THEY COULD GET AIDS FROM ELEVATOR
BUTTONS, SWIMMING POOLS, OR SUBWAY STRAPS.

IN ACTUALITY, AIDS WAS ONLY SPREAD THROUGH BODILY FLUIDS
LIKE BLOOD AND SEMEN (NOT SALIVA), BUT WITHOUT ANY
PUBLIC EDUCATION MOST PEOPLE HAD NO IDEA.

AS THE DECADE PROGRESSED—AND AIDS FATALITIES ROSE—

THE STIGMA AND FEAR SURROUNDING
THE DISEASE ONLY INCREASED.

DOCTORS AND NURSES ROUTINELY REFUSED TO TREAT
AIDS PATIENTS, POLITICANS TALKED ABOUT THE ILLNESS AS
A SELF-INFLICTED MORAL FAILING, AND 1 IN 7 AMERICANS
APPROVED OF FORCING PEOPLE WITH AIDS TO
GET TATTOOED TO IDENTIFY THEM.

THE REAGAN ADMINISTRATION
DIDN'T ADDRESS THE
EPIDEMIC IN EARNEST UNTIL
1987, SPENDING THE MAJORITY
OF THE DECADE TREATING IT
LIKE A JOKE DURING PRESS
BRIEFINGS AND DEFLECTING
IT AS A MORAL ISSUE.

"AFTER ALL,
WHEN IT COMES TO
PREVENTING AIDS, DON'T
MEDICINE AND MORALITY
TEACH THE SAME LESSONS?"

ACT UP, FIGHT B[ACK]

CONDOMS NOT COFFINS, AIDS WON'T WAIT

PEOPLE LIVING WITH AIDS AND THOSE WHO LOVED THEM REFUSED TO BE TREATED LIKE SINFUL PARIAHS WHO DESERVED AN EARLY DEATH. SO THEY STARTED MEETING UP TO FIGURE OUT HOW TO CHANGE THE PUBLIC'S PERCEPTION AND DEMAND MORE HUMANE, EFFECTIVE TREATMENT AND CARE.

IN 1987 THEY FORMED ACT UP— THE AIDS COALITION TO UNLEASH POWER— "A DIVERSE, NONPARTISAN GROUP OF INDIVIDUALS UNITED IN ANGER AND COMMITTED TO DIRECT ACTION TO END THE AIDS CRISIS."

CHAPTERS SPRANG UP ACROSS THE COUNTRY. IN NEW YORK CITY, ACT UP MEETINGS WERE HELD EVERY MONDAY NIGHT. THE RAUCOUS, ENRAGED, JOYFUL, COOL, RADICALLY DEMOCRATIC GATHERINGS ENCOURAGED ALL WHO ATTENDED TO BRING THEIR SKILLS AND CREATIVITY AND LIVED EXPERIENCE AND GRIEF TO THE FIGHT.

CE, AIDS ACTION NOW

CK, FIGHT AIDS

THE GROUP QUICKLY BECAME KNOWN FOR ITS BRAZENLY CREATIVE ACTIONS, BOLD GRAPHICS, AND BITING CHANTS THAT DEMANDED ATTENTION.

ACT UP MEMBERS POPPED UP EVERYWHERE FROM THE WHITE HOUSE TO TRUMP TOWER TO COSMOPOLITAN MAGAZINE'S OFFICES.

THEY INFILTRATED THE NEW YORK STOCK EXCHANGE, CHAINING THEMSELVES INSIDE TO PROTEST THE ASTRONOMICAL PRICE OF AZT (AN ANTI-HIV DRUG). THEY STAGED A DIE-IN DURING MASS AT ST. PATRICK'S CATHEDRAL TO PROTEST THE CHURCH'S ANTI-GAY, ANTI-SAFE SEX STANCES—LYING DOWN IN THE AISLES, AND CHANTING—WHILE 5,000 PEOPLE, SOME DRESSED AS CONDOMS, PROTESTED OUTSIDE.

THE ACTIONS WORKED.

ACT UP REPEATEDLY MADE NATIONAL NEWS, GOT THE PRICE OF AZT LOWERED, AND SECURED MEETINGS WITH GOVERNMENT OFFICIALS LIKE ANTHONY FAUCI, THE HEAD OF THE NATIONAL INSTITUTE OF ALLERGY AND INFECTIOUS DISEASES.

BUT, BY EARLY 1990,
AZT WAS STILL THE
ONLY AVAILABLE DRUG
(AND IT WAS CONTROVERSIAL),
MEETINGS HAD STALLED,
AND PEOPLE JUST KEPT
GETTING SICKER
AND DYING.

FRUSTRATED, ACT UP
DECIDED TO GO TO THE
NATIONAL INSTITUTES
OF HEALTH
TO DEMAND THAT MORE DRUGS
BE TESTED, RELEASED, AND
MADE WIDELY AVAILABLE
AT A MUCH FASTER RATE,
WITH MORE TRANSPARENCY,
AND IN COLLABORATION WITH THE DIVERSE ARRAY
OF PEOPLE WHO WERE ACTUALLY LIVING WITH
AND DYING FROM THE DISEASE.

THE GROUP CALLED THE ACTION
"STORM THE NIH"
AND ENLISTED ACT UP CHAPTERS FROM AROUND THE COUNTRY
TO MEET IN BETHESDA, MARYLAND, ON MAY 21, 1990.

THE EVENT TOOK A MASSIVE AMOUNT OF LOGISTICAL PLANNING— SECURING BUSES, MOTEL ROOMS, A PA SYSTEM, WALKIE-TALKIES, AND MEGAPHONES; DESIGNING AND WRITING AND PRODUCING FLYERS AND POSTERS AND LETTERS AND ADS; LINING UP MEDICAL AND LEGAL SUPPORT, A MEDIA TABLE, A SAFE ZONE FOR DISABLED MEMBERS— ALL OF WHICH WAS EXECUTED AT AN ORGANIZATION-WIDE LEVEL FROM THE TOP DOWN.

BUT IT ALSO REQUIRED A
TREMENDOUS AMOUNT OF
CREATIVE PLANNING,
WHICH WAS TAKEN ON IN A MUCH MORE
ORGANIC, COLLECTIVE WAY.

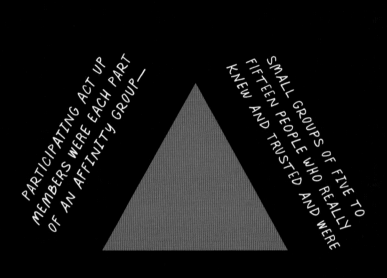

PARTICIPATING ACT UP MEMBERS WERE EACH PART OF AN AFFINITY GROUP—

SMALL GROUPS OF FIVE TO FIFTEEN PEOPLE WHO REALLY KNEW AND TRUSTED AND WERE

RESPONSIBLE
FOR ONE ANOTHER.

THEY DESIGNED AND EXECUTED THEIR ACTIONS INDEPENDENTLY OF
THE LARGER ORGANIZATION, EACH WITH CREATIVE NAMES LIKE

CHER!, THE JUICERS, THE MARYS,
CHAIN GANG, POWER TOOLS, W.A.R.,

AND EACH CREATED AN
ATTENTION-GRABBING SPECTACLE
TO RAISE AWARENESS FOR A
HIGHLY SPECIFIC PROBLEM.

THE MORNING OF THE ACTION, 1,500 ACT UP MEMBERS MARCHED ONTO THE NIH CAMPUS IN AN OVERWHELMING CACOPHANY OF BANNERS AND BELLS AND DRUMS AND CHANTS.

ONE GROUP SET OFF AIR RAID SIRENS EVERY TWELVE MINUTES TO REPRESENT HOW OFTEN PEOPLE WERE DYING OF AIDS IN THE U.S.

ONE GROUP DESIGNED A GRAVEYARD WITH TOMBSTONES WITH THE EPITAPHS "DEAD FROM HOMOPHOBIA" AND "BURIED UNDER RED TAPE" TO HIGHLIGHT HOW BIGOTRY AND BUREAUCRACY WERE CONTRIBUTORS TO THE CRISIS.

ONE GROUP CREATED A LONG SNAKE WHOSE HEAD READ: "AIDS IS MORE THAN ONE DISEASE" AND LISTED THE NAMES OF RELATED OPPORTUNISTIC INFECTIONS THAT NEEDED ATTENTION LIKE TUBERCULOSIS AND ENCEPHALOPATHY.

ONE GROUP COVERED THEIR FACES IN BANDAGES LIKE THE INVISIBLE MAN AND CHANTED "NIH IS A DISASTER, WOMEN DIE SIX TIMES FASTER" AND "YOU TEST MICE WHILE WOMEN DIE" TO DRAW ATTENTION TO THE FACT THAT AIDS WASN'T KILLING ONLY MEN, AND YET NO WOMEN WERE INCLUDED IN CLINICAL TRIALS.

ONE GROUP FINAGLED THEIR WAY INTO THE OFFICE OF DAN HOTH (THE DIRECTOR OF THE NIH'S AIDS DIVISION) AND **SLIPPED FACT SHEETS** ABOUT WHAT THE AIDS CLINICAL TRIAL GROUPS NEEDED TO STUDY INTO EVERY FILE FOLDER THEY COULD FIND.

THERE WAS ALSO A PLANNED PICKET,

CIVIL DISOBEDIENCE,

AND MADE-FOR-MEDIA MOMENTS,

LIKE A GROUP RUNNING THROUGH THE CROWD WITH COLORED SMOKE CANISTERS ON TWELVE-FOOT POLES, CREATING

A GIANT, RAINBOW PLUME ACROSS THE SKY.

EACH ACTION WAS CRAFTED FOR

MAXIMAL MEDIA ATTENTION—

MEMBERS HONED SOUNDBITES,
PROVIDED LOCAL ANGLES,
AND FILMED THEIR ACTIONS.

A MONTH AFTER STORM THE NIH,
FAUCI ANNOUNCED THAT AIDS CLINICAL
TRIAL GROUPS AND THE NIH WOULD RESPOND

TO ACT UP'S DEMANDS.

GOING FORWARD THERE WOULD BE

PATIENT ADVOCATES

ON EVERY DRUG TESTING COMMITTEE,
AND TRIALS EXPANDED TO INCLUDE

WOMEN, PEOPLE OF COLOR, DRUG USERS, AND CHILDREN.

IT WAS A HUGE STEP.

AND ONE THAT CHANGED THE COURSE OF
HOW DRUG TESTING AND DEVELOPMENT
WORKED FAR BEYOND AIDS.

STILL, MANY PEOPLE WITH AIDS
STRUGGLED TO SECURE
TREATMENT AND SUPPORT.

SINCE THE CDC'S DEFINITION OF AIDS
WAS BASED ON HOW THE DISEASE
PRESENTED ITSELF IN WHITE MEN,
MANY WOMEN AND OTHERS WHO DIDN'T HAVE
THE SAME SYMPTOMS COULDN'T GET OFFICIALLY
CLASSIFIED AS HAVING AIDS,
AND THEREFORE COULDN'T ACCESS
BENEFITS AND TREATMENTS.

SO ACT UP'S MEMBERS KEPT
AGITATING FOR CHANGE—
THROUGH EDUCATION,
ACTIONS, AND LAWSUITS.

KATRINA HASLIP, A BLACK MUSLIM WOMAN
WITH AIDS, FOUNDED AIDS COUNSELING AND
EDUCATION (ACE) WHILE INCARCERATED TO
SUPPORT, EDUCATE, AND FIGHT
FOR OTHER WOMEN STRUGGLING WITH THE DISEASE
(AND THE ISOLATION AND OPPRESSION THEIR
DIAGNOSES BROUGHT).

SHE AND IRIS DE LA CRUZ, A FELLOW ACE MEMBER,
SEX WORKER, AND DRUG USER, LED AN ACT UP
PROTEST AT HEALTH AND HUMAN SERVICES IN
OCTOBER 1990, WHILE ALSO ACTING AS PLAINTIFFS
IN AN ASSOCIATED LAWSUIT AGAINST THE CDC.

IT TOOK ANOTHER SIX YEARS BEFORE
HAART, THE FIRST DRUG COCKTAIL THAT TURNED
AIDS INTO A CHRONIC, MANAGEABLE
CONDITION, WAS DISCOVERED.

ACT UP ACTIONS GREW
INCREASINGLY DEVASTATING,
INCLUDING PUBLICLY CARRYING THE BODIES
OF BELOVED MEMBERS THROUGH THE STREETS IN
MASSIVE POLITICAL FUNERALS,
AND DUMPING THE ASHES OF LOVED ONES
ON THE LAWN OF THE WHITE HOUSE.

DEATHS DROPPED RAPIDLY IN THE U.S. AFTER 1996,
BUT THE DRUGS STILL WEREN'T
ACCESSIBLE TO EVERYONE.

BY 1998, BLACK PEOPLE
ACCOUNTED FOR 49 PERCENT OF
AIDS-RELATED DEATHS, ALMOST
TEN TIMES
THE MORTALITY RATE
OF WHITE PEOPLE.

WORLDWIDE, THE CRISIS ALSO GREW, NOT HITTING ITS PEAK UNTIL 2004.

IN 2020, 690,000 PEOPLE WERE STILL DYING OF AIDS-RELATED ILLNESSES WORLDWIDE.

"WHAT AIDS REVEALED WAS NOT THE PROBLEM OF THE VIRUS, WHAT AIDS REVEALED WERE THE **PROBLEMS OF SOCIETY,**" SAID ACT UP MEMBER AND ARTIST ZOE LEONARD IN AN ORAL HISTORY. "IT WAS THIS FISSURE THROUGH WHICH EVERYTHING, ALL THE WAYS IN WHICH OUR SOCIETY ISN'T WORKING, BECAME

REALLY

CLEAR."

September 30

...DV...
and tran...
...America, were safe arrived at Nan-...
...bout 900 troops, collected from several...
...harbour, having very narrowly...
...reck on the back of Cape Cod,...
...ould have left the extensive...
America, almost bare of...
...s, but in no worse...
...fortresses and...
...ions had

...l of war
...Halifax, with
Early this morning a number of boats
were observed round the town, making
soundings, &c.—At 3 o'clock in the after-
noon, the Launceston of 40 guns, the Mer-
maid of 38, Glasgow 20, the Beaver 14,
Senegal 14, Bonetta 10, several armed
schooners, which together with the Romney
of 60 guns, and the other ships of war before
in the harbour, all commanded by Capt.
Smith, came up to town, bringing with
them, the 14th Regiment, Col. Dalr...
and 29th Regiment, Col. Carr...

GIVE ME
LIBERTY

"WHOEVER CONTROLS THE MEDIA, CONTROLS THE MIND."

—JIM MORRISON

IN THE FALL OF 1768,
BRITISH WARSHIPS SAILED INTO BOSTON HARBOR,
UNLOADED BRITISH SOLDIERS,
AND PUT THE CITY UNDER MILITARY RULE.

THE OCCUPATION WAS INTENDED TO
QUELL THE GROWING UNREST
OVER THE TOWNSHEND ACTS, WHICH HAD IMPOSED
UNPOPULAR IMPORT TAXES ON EVERYTHING
FROM PAPER TO GLASS THE YEAR BEFORE.

WITHIN A MONTH OF THE SOLDIERS' ARRIVAL,
A WEEKLY COLUMN STARTED CIRCULATING IN NEWSPAPERS
THROUGHOUT THE COLONIES.

CALLED THE "JOURNAL OF OCCURRENCES,"
IT READ LIKE A DIARY, FEATURING SHORT ACCOUNTS OF
WHAT WAS HAPPENING IN OCCUPIED BOSTON.

The BOSTON   Evening-Poſt.

Containing the freſheſt & moſt important   Advices, Foreign and Domeſtick.

September 28, 1768 [1]

ADVICE received that the men of war and transports from Halifax, with about 900 troops, collected from several parts of America, were safe arrived at Nantasket Harbour,

October 29

The inhabitants of this town have been of late greatly insulted and abused by some of the officers and soldiers,

November 11

What an appearance does Boston now make! One of the first commercial towns in America, has now several regiments of soldiers quartered in the midst of it,

AS TIME PASSED, THE ALLEGED ATROCITIES COMMITTED BY THE BRITISH
PILED UP. STORIES OF DRUNKEN SOLDIERS, UNLAWFUL SEARCHES,
ASSAULTED WOMEN, CRYING CHILDREN, COMPLICIT CITIZENS.

THE ACCOUNTS CLAIMED TO BE "STRICTLY FACT,"
BUT WERE (MOST LIKELY) GREATLY EXAGGERATED—
INTENTIONALLY CRAFTED TO STOKE RESENTMENT
AND APPEAL TO COLONISTS' FEAR.

IT WORKED.

THE JOURNAL WAS WILDLY POPULAR, AND ITS CLAIMS ENRAGED THE COLONISTS. NO ONE KNOWS FOR SURE WHO WAS BEHIND IT—THE ACCOUNTS WERE ANONYMOUS—BUT HISTORIANS OFTEN CREDIT SAMUEL ADAMS AS PLAYING A MAJOR ROLE.

SAM ADAMS, THE COUSIN OF FUTURE SECOND PRESIDENT JOHN ADAMS, HAD A REPUTATION FOR BEING A RADICAL AND AGITATOR IN THE COLONIES. HE WAS CONVINCED THAT THE COLONISTS WERE VICTIMS OF A VAST BRITISH CONSPIRACY TO STRIP THEM OF THEIR LIBERTY AND ENSLAVE THEM, AND HE WAS THE FIRST POPULAR LEADER TO CALL FOR INDEPENDENCE.

ADAMS KNEW THE ONLY WAY HIS VIEWS WOULD BECOME MAINSTREAM WAS THROUGH THE SUPPORT OF ORDINARY PEOPLE. SO HE SET OUT TO CONVINCE THEM.

HE PERSUADED AND PRODDED AND PROPAGANDIZED VIA EVERY MEDIUM AT HIS DISPOSAL— SPEECHES IN TOWN HALLS, DISCUSSIONS AT TAVERNS, ARTICLES IN BROADSIDES, LEAFLETS, PAMPHLETS, NEWSPAPERS.

HE BELIEVED EVERY SUCCESSIVE
BRITISH ACTION CONFIRMED
HIS THEORIES, AND
RAILED AGAINST
EACH ONE—

THE STAMP ACT

"a deep-laid and desperate plan of imperial despotism has been laid, and partly executed, for the extinction of all civil liberty."

THE SUGAR ACT

"are we not reduced from the Character of free Subjects to the miserable State of tributary Slaves?"

THE OCCUPATION

"secretly intended to introduce a general massacre."

THE TOWNSHEND ACTS (AND GOV. BERNARD)

"a scourge to this Province, a curse to North America, and a plague on the whole Empire."

THE BRITISH, OF COURSE,
DENIED THE ALLEGATIONS,
CLAIMING THE TAXES WERE LEVIED
TO OFFSET THE COST OF
PROTECTING THE COLONIES.

LOYALISTS AND TORIES CLAIMED ADAMS WAS THE ONE
WHO WAS SPARKING THE HOSTILITIES, CALLING HIM A

"GRAND INCENDIARY."

THEY REFERRED TO THE BOSTON RESISTANCE AS
ADAMS'S CONSPIRACY
AND AMERICAN PATRIOTS AS
ADAMS'S CREW.

ABOVE ALL THEY LOATHED THE
POWERFUL EFFECT OF HIS WRITING—
"EVERY DIP OF HIS PEN, STUNG LIKE A
HORNED SNAKE." —GOVERNOR BERNARD

COLONIAL MOB VIOLENCE RATCHETED UP,
SUCKING THE ANGER OFF THE PAGE
AND SPEWING IT INTO THE STREET.

COLONISTS BOYCOTTED BRITISH
BUSINESSES, DESTROYED THE PRESSES
OF LOYALIST PRINTERS, AND RANSACKED
THE HOMES OF BRITISH LEADERS.

ON MARCH 5, 1770, THE SIMMERING TENSIONS FAMOUSLY CAME TO A ROLLING BOIL AT THE DOOR OF THE CUSTOMS HOUSE ON KING STREET.

HUNDREDS OF PATRIOTS GATHERED, CHUCKING SNOWBALLS, STICKS, STONES, AND BOTTLES AT BRITISH SOLDIERS, DARING THEM TO SHOOT BACK.

WHEN THEY FINALLY DID, FIVE COLONISTS LAY DEAD IN THE SNOW.

ADAMS BRANDED IT THE BOSTON MASSACRE, AND HIS LURID DESCRIPTIONS OF INNOCENT MEN "WALLOWING IN THEIR GORE" EFFECTIVELY LAID THE GROUNDWORK FOR THE AMERICAN REVOLUTION.

BUTCHER'S HALL

CUSTOM HOUSE

Engrav'd Printed & Sold by PAUL REVERE BOSTON

CONTEMPORARY HISTORIANS AGREE
THERE WAS NEVER A PLOT TO
ENSLAVE THE COLONIES.

THE COLONISTS, HOWEVER,
DID ENSLAVE BLACK PEOPLE.
AND WOULD CONTINUE TO DO SO FOR
NEARLY ONE HUNDRED MORE YEARS.

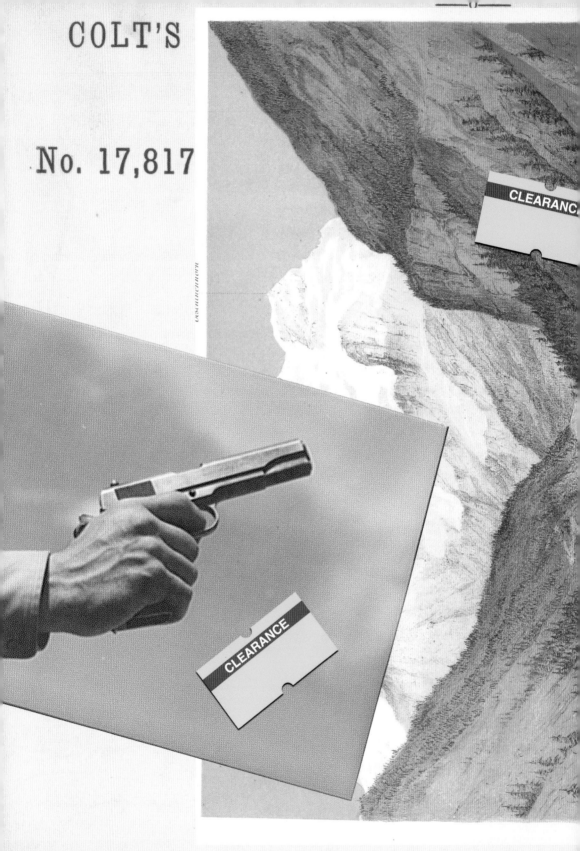

COLT'S

No. 17,817

GOOD GUY WITH A GUN

"RIDIN' THE RANGE ONCE MORE, TOTIN' MY OLD .44"

—LYRICS FROM GENE AUTRY'S "BACK IN THE SADDLE AGAIN"

BY 1860, WHEN THE WORLD PICTURED AN "AMERICAN"

MANY SAW SAM COLT.

THE MASSIVELY WEALTHY GUN INVENTOR AND MANUFACTURER
WAS WELL-KNOWN BOTH AT HOME AND ABROAD
FOR HIS PRODUCTS AND HIS PERSONALITY:

OPPORTUNISTIC

CHARMING

GENIUS

BRASH

ABRASIVE

PRACTICAL

OVERCONFIDENT

FAST-TALKING

IMAGINATIVE

MERCENARY

COLONEL COLT.

COLT WASN'T THE FIRST
AMERICAN GUN MANUFACTURER, OR
EVEN THE FIRST TO INVENT THE REVOLVER
HE IS CREDITED WITH POPULARIZING. HIS
SUCCESS CAME FROM HIS ABILITY TO SELL—HE WAS

A RELENTLESS, MASTER MARKETER.

COLT KNEW HOW TO PUT ON A SHOW FROM A VERY YOUNG AGE.

AT FOURTEEN, HE PRINTED POSTERS AROUND HIS SCHOOL INVITING CLASSMATES TO SEE HIM "BLOW A RAFT SKY-HIGH" USING UNDERWATER EXPLOSIVES. AT EIGHTEEN, HE DUBBED HIMSELF "DR. COULT OF NEW YORK, LONDON, AND CALCUTTA" AND TRAVELED AROUND GIVING NITROUS OXIDE DEMONSTRATIONS TO EXCITED CROWDS FOR A FEE.

HIS EARLY CAREER WAS LITTERED WITH BUSINESS FAILURES— HE BLEW THROUGH FAMILY MONEY, CREATED FAULTY PROTOTYPES, AND SHUTTERED A FACTORY, ALL BEFORE THE AGE OF TWENTY-SEVEN.

BUT BUSINESS FINALLY TURNED AROUND WHEN COLT MANAGED TO GET SAM WALKER, A FAMOUS TEXAS RANGER, TO PRAISE HIS PATERSON REVOLVER IN 1846.

"WITH IMPROVEMENTS I THINK THEY CAN BE RENDERED THE MOST PERFECT WEAPON IN THE WORLD," WALKER WROTE, "...TO KEEP THE VARIOUS WARLIKE TRIBES OF INDIANS AND MEXICANS IN SUBJECTION."

COLT CAPITALIZED ON WALKER'S TESTIMONIAL.

TOGETHER THEY DEVELOPED THE COLT WALKER, AND COLT SOLD 1,000 OF THEM TO THE U.S. GOVERNMENT TO USE IN THE MEXICAN-AMERICAN WAR.

BEFORE COLT'S
REVOLVERS,
HANDGUNS
WERE
EXPENSIVE,
INACCURATE,
AND
CUMBERSOME
TO RELOAD.

COLT MADE THE GUNS
MORE PRECISE
AND ADDED A REVOLVING
CHAMBER THAT ALLOWED
SOLDIERS TO GET FIVE OR
SIX SHOTS OFF IN A ROW
WITHOUT RELOADING.

SOLDIERS LOVED THE GUNS,
AND COLT CONTINUED TO
**SECURE GOVERMENT
CONTRACTS FOR
BIG ORDERS,**
BOTH IN THE U.S. AND ABROAD.

HE BUILT A MASSIVE 200-ACRE
ARMORY IN HARTFORD, CONNECTICUT,
CALLED "COLTSVILLE" TO KEEP UP
WITH THE DEMAND AND STREAMLINED
MASS PRODUCTION USING
INTERCHANGEABLE PARTS
HALF A CENTURY BEFORE HENRY FORD.

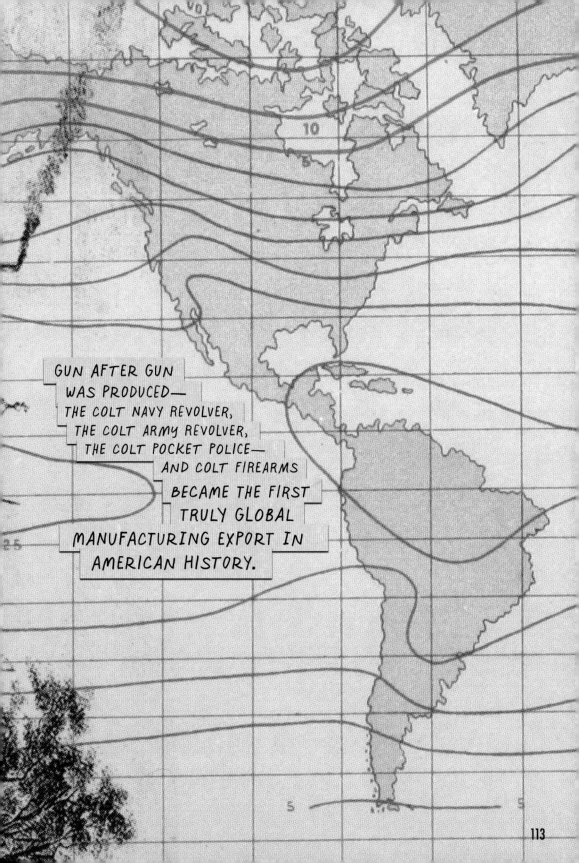

GUN AFTER GUN
WAS PRODUCED—
THE COLT NAVY REVOLVER,
THE COLT ARMY REVOLVER,
THE COLT POCKET POLICE—
AND COLT FIREARMS
BECAME THE FIRST
TRULY GLOBAL
MANUFACTURING EXPORT IN
AMERICAN HISTORY.

WITH HIS ASSEMBLY LINE AND STEADY STREAM OF GOVERNMENT CONTRACTS SUBSIDIZING PRODUCTION, COLT WAS ABLE TO MAKE HIS GUNS AFFORDABLE FOR INDIVIDUALS AS WELL.

THE TERM **"MANIFEST DESTINY"** HAD JUST APPEARED IN PRINT, AND AMERICANS WERE **PUSHING WEST.**

COLT INTENTIONALLY TIED HIS GUNS TO A **FRONTIER IDENTITY—** DARING, RUGGED, WHITE, MALE.

HE MARKETED THEM TO MEN HEADING TO STRIKE IT RICH IN THE GOLD RUSH AND SETTLERS LOOKING TO DEFEND THE LAND THEY STOLE FROM NATIVE PEOPLES.

IN THE PROCESS, HE DEVELOPED MODERN SALES AND BRANDING TECHNIQUES.

COLT...

CLEARANCE
DEVELOPED THE NOTION OF **"NEW AND IMPROVED"**

CLEARANCE
INVESTED IN **DESIGN**

CLEARANCE
INVENTED THE **USER MANUAL**

CLEARANCE
UNDERCUT THE COMPETITION **ON PRICING**

Entered according to act of Congress. A. 1867, by Currier & I

THE PION

ON THE WI

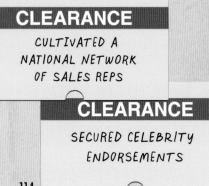

CLEARANCE
CULTIVATED A NATIONAL NETWORK OF SALES REPS

CLEARANCE
SECURED CELEBRITY ENDORSEMENTS

114

BRANDED HIMSELF, FINAGLING AN HONORARY COMMISSION OF "COLONEL"

IN 1857, HE EVEN COMMISSIONED POPULAR ARTIST GEORGE CATLIN TO PAINT COLTS INTO HIS FRONTIER SCENES.

PAID PRODUCT PLACEMENT

IT WORKED. BETWEEN 1850 AND 1860, COLT SOLD 170,000 "POCKET" AND "BELT" REVOLVERS MAINLY TO CIVILIANS IN THE "WILD WEST."

rks Office of the District Court of the United S

EER'S

ERN FRONT

115

AS THE CIVIL WAR RAMPED UP, COLT CONTINUED SELLING GUNS TO ANYONE WHO WANTED TO BUY THEM— NORTH OR SOUTH.

AND HIS GUNS WERE

HIGHLY COVETED.

"WE WERE ALL FESTOONED WITH REVOLVERS. I CARRIED FOUR OF COLT'S, TWO IN MY BELT AND TWO ON MY SADDLE HOLSTERS BUT THIS WAS BY NO MEANS AN EXCESS."

—ANONYMOUS UNION SOLDIER

COLT NEVER SAW THE WAR END.
HE DIED IN 1862 AT FORTY-SEVEN.

HIS OBITUARY EXPLODED
WITH PRAISE:

"Emphatically the architect of his own fortunes"

"ALMOST A MIDAS"

"PUBLIC-SPIRITED CITIZEN"

IT'S ESTIMATED THAT DURING HIS LIFETIME,
COLT OVERSAW THE PRODUCTION OF
400,000 FIREARMS.

THE COUNTRY'S APPETITE FOR ARMS
(IN LARGE PART THANKS TO COLT)
GREW ALONGSIDE HIS SUCCESS—
FROM 1830 TO 1850,
WILLS MENTIONING GUN OWNERSHIP
ROSE BY 50 PERCENT.

THE MOST ICONIC COLT GUN,
    THE SINGLE ACTION ARMY,
WASN'T EVEN INVENTED UNTIL TEN YEARS AFTER COLT'S DEATH.

POPULARLY KNOWN AS THE COLT .45 OR THE
"PEACEMAKER,"
IT BECAME THE UNITED STATES CAVALRY'S OFFICIAL SIDEARM
THROUGHOUT THE INDIAN WARS—
THE APACHE WARS, THE UTE WARS,
    THE SIOUX WARS, THE NEZ PERCE
        WAR, THE CROW WAR.

BY 1890, THE U.S. GOVERNMENT HAD PURCHASED
OVER 37,000 PEACEMAKERS
AND THE FRONTIER WAS
DECLARED "CLOSED."

THE NATIONS THAT U.S. SOLDIERS HAD USED THESE GUNS AGAINST –
INCLUDING THE COMANCHE, THE LAKOTA, THE DINÉ, THE OJIBWE –
HAD BEEN DRIVEN FROM THEIR LANDS AND ONTO RESERVATIONS.

VERSIONS OF THE COLT .45
CONTINUED TO BE USED BY THE U.S. ARMY
THROUGHOUT THE 20TH CENTURY—
IN WORLD WAR I, WORLD WAR II,
THE KOREAN WAR, THE WAR IN VIETNAM.

COLT GUNS ALSO FOUND THEIR WAY

OUT OF THE REAL WORLD
AND ONTO THE SCREEN

AS THE AMERICAN MOVIE AND TELEVISION INDUSTRIES GREW.

GANGSTERS, DETECTIVES,
COWBOYS, COPS—
ALL CARRIED GUNS,
AND MANY CARRIED COLTS.

TODAY, THERE ARE MORE GUNS
THAN PEOPLE IN THE UNITED STATES,
ACCOUNTING FOR NEARLY
HALF OF ALL CIVILIAN-HELD FIREARMS
IN THE WORLD.

GUN TECHNOLOGY HAS
MOVED FAR BEYOND
COLT'S ORIGINAL
REVOLVERS.

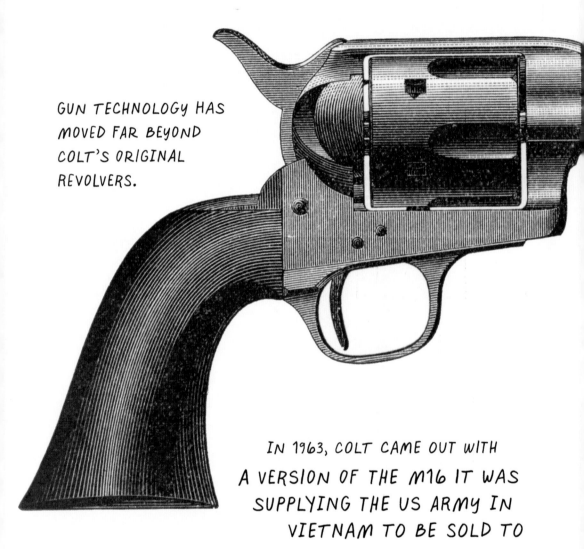

IN 1963, COLT CAME OUT WITH
A VERSION OF THE M16 IT WAS
SUPPLYING THE US ARMY IN
VIETNAM TO BE SOLD TO
CIVILIANS AND POLICE DEPARTMENTS—

A SEMI-AUTOMATIC AR-15.

AR-15S CAN EASILY FIRE TWENTY OR THIRTY ROUNDS AT A TIME, AND EACH AR-15 BULLET CARRIES THREE TIMES MORE ENERGY THAN A HANDGUN, EARNING IT THE EPITHET

THE PERFECT KILLING MACHINE.

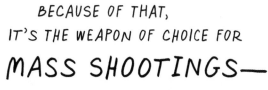

BECAUSE OF THAT, IT'S THE WEAPON OF CHOICE FOR

MASS SHOOTINGS—

FROM AN ELEMENTARY SCHOOL IN SANDY HOOK TO A HIGH SCHOOL IN PARKLAND TO A SUPERMARKET IN BUFFALO TO A MOVIE THEATER IN AURORA TO A NIGHTCLUB IN ORLANDO.

THE MASS SHOOTERS ARE NEARLY ALL MEN.

ONE OUT OF EVERY FIVE FIREARMS PURCHASED IN THE U.S. TODAY IS AN AR-STYLE RIFLE.

HUNDREDS OF MANUFACTURERS PRODUCE SLEWS OF VARIATIONS WITH NAMES LIKE "PATRIOT DEFENSE," "COMBAT PROTECTOR," "FREEDOM RIFLE," AND "INDEPENDENCE."

IT IS, AS THE NATIONAL RIFLE ASSOCIATION STATES,

"AMERICA'S RIFLE."

A NEW WORLD

"INVISIBLE THINGS ARE NOT NECESSARILY 'NOT THERE,'
CERTAIN ABSENCES ARE SO STRESSED, SO ORNATE, SO PLANNED,
THEY CALL ATTENTION TO THEMSELVES."

—TONI MORRISON

AFTER CHRISTOPHER COLUMBUS RETURNED TO SPAIN IN 1493 LOADED WITH NEWS—

OF ABUNDANCE,

OF SPLENDOR,

OF A WEAPONLESS, WELCOMING PEOPLE—

A SLEW OF EXPLORERS SET OUT TO EXPLOIT THE "NEW" WORLD HE HAD "DISCOVERED."

THEIR NAMES ARE WELL-KNOWN—

CORONADO, CORTÉS, DE SOTO, DE LEON, DE BALBOA.

CHRISTIAN, EUROPEAN MEN.

BUT THE FIRST NON-NATIVE TO EXPLORE THE PRESENT-DAY AMERICAN SOUTHWEST WASN'T CHRISTIAN, WASN'T EUROPEAN, AND DIDN'T SET OUT BY HIS OWN FREE WILL.

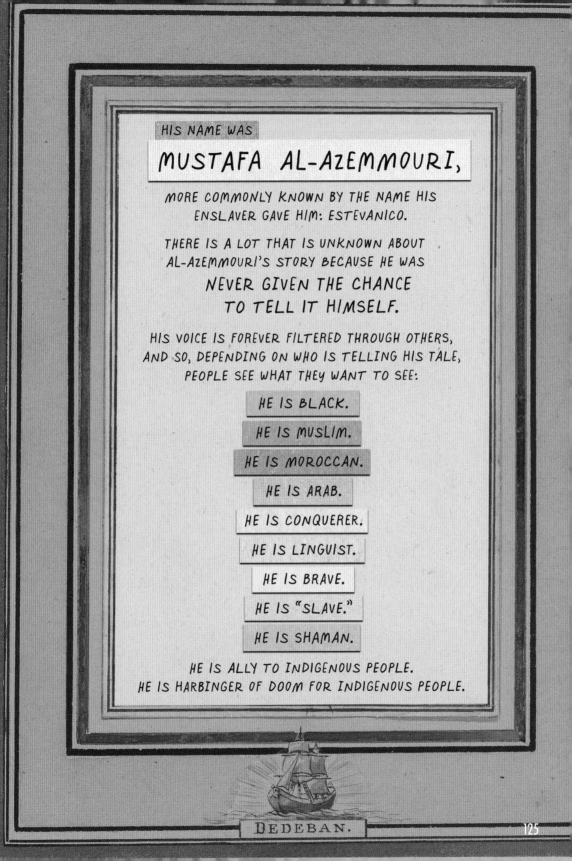

HIS NAME WAS

MUSTAFA AL-AZEMMOURI,

MORE COMMONLY KNOWN BY THE NAME HIS
ENSLAVER GAVE HIM: ESTEVANICO.

THERE IS A LOT THAT IS UNKNOWN ABOUT
AL-AZEMMOURI'S STORY BECAUSE HE WAS
**NEVER GIVEN THE CHANCE
TO TELL IT HIMSELF.**

HIS VOICE IS FOREVER FILTERED THROUGH OTHERS,
AND SO, DEPENDING ON WHO IS TELLING HIS TALE,
PEOPLE SEE WHAT THEY WANT TO SEE:

HE IS BLACK.

HE IS MUSLIM.

HE IS MOROCCAN.

HE IS ARAB.

HE IS CONQUERER.

HE IS LINGUIST.

HE IS BRAVE.

HE IS "SLAVE."

HE IS SHAMAN.

HE IS ALLY TO INDIGENOUS PEOPLE.
HE IS HARBINGER OF DOOM FOR INDIGENOUS PEOPLE.

DEDEBAN.

MOST OF WHAT IS KNOWN ABOUT AL-AZEMMOURI'S LIFE IS FROM A SHORT BOOK CALLED NAUFRAGIOS, OR **SHIPWRECKED,** WRITTEN BY ALVAR NÚÑEZ CABEZA DE VACA IN 1542.

ON JUNE 17, 1527,

THE NARVÁEZ EXPEDITION—

FIVE SHIPS CARRYING 600 PEOPLE, INCLUDING NOBLES, SOLDIERS, SERVANTS, SPOUSES, PEOPLE THEY ENSLAVED, HORSES— SET SAIL FROM THE PORT OF SANLÚCAR DE BARRAMEDA IN SPAIN.

ITS MISSION WAS TO ESTABLISH

A COLONY IN "LA FLORIDA"

(WHAT IS NOW FLORIDA, AND ALL LANDS TO THE NORTH AND WEST, INCLUDING NORTHERN MEXICO), AND CLAIM THE LAND FOR KING CHARLES.

IT FAILED. THE ENTIRE EXPEDITION WAS DISASTER AFTER DISASTER—HURRICANES, DISEASE, RAIDS, STARVATION, LOST SHIPS, AIMLESS WANDERING. THEY LOST HOPE, ATE THEIR HORSES, ATE EACH OTHER.

BY 1532, ONLY FOUR PEOPLE WERE LEFT,
STRANDED IN COAHUILTECAN LANDS
(WHAT IS NOW KNOWN AS TEXAS)—

DE VACA, ALONSO DEL CASTILLO MALDONADO,
ANDRÉS DORANTES DE CARRANZA,
AND THE MAN DORANTES CLAIMED OWNERSHIP OF,
MUSTAFA AL-AZEMMOURI.

SHIPWRECKED SPANS MORE THAN EIGHT YEARS, AND WITHIN THAT
TIME THE GROUP OF FOUR SURVIVORS GO FROM BEING CASTAWAYS
KEPT ALIVE BY THE KINDESS OF THE PEOPLE THEY ENCOUNTER,
TO BECOMING ENSLAVED BY THE KARANKAWA, TO ESCAPING AND
EMERGING AS RENOWNED CHRISTIAN FAITH HEALERS WHO TRAVEL
VILLAGE TO VILLAGE PERFORMING MIRACULOUS CURES—
IN ONE CASE, DE VACA CLAIMS TO
RAISE SOMEONE FROM THE DEAD.

THEIR REPUTATION GROWS AND THE FOUR ARE SHOWERED WITH
GIFTS OF THANKS—ANIMAL SKINS, BEADS, GOURDS, FEATHERS.

THEY MAKE THEIR WAY ACROSS THE SOUTHWEST, AND BY THE TIME THEY
STUMBLE INTO OTHER CHRISTIANOS IN NORTHERN MEXICO IN 1536,

THEY'VE AMASSED A DEDICATED FOLLOWING.

ACCORDING TO DE VACA, AT LEAST.

DE VACA'S TALE STARS DE VACA, AND IS TOLD AS
A LETTER TO THE KING—AN EXPLANATION AND EXCUSE
FOR WHY THEY FAILED (AND WHY DE VACA, AS TREASURER
OF THE EXPEDITION, ISN'T BRINGING BACK ANY RICHES).

OF THE FOUR, AL-AZEMMOURI IS
PLACED DEEPEST IN THE BACKGROUND,
BUT EVEN AS DE VACA SHOVES HIM
OFFSTAGE, WHEN HE DOES APPEAR
THE IMPORTANCE OF HIS

CRITICAL ROLES—
AS SCOUT, AS EMISSARY,
AS MEDIATOR—

SLIPS THROUGH.

"THE BLACK MAN
ALWAYS SPOKE
TO THEM AND
INFORMED
HIMSELF ABOUT
THE ROADS WE
WISHED TO
TRAVEL AND
THE VILLAGERS
THAT THERE WERE
AND ABOUT THE
OTHER THINGS
WE WANTED
TO KNOW."

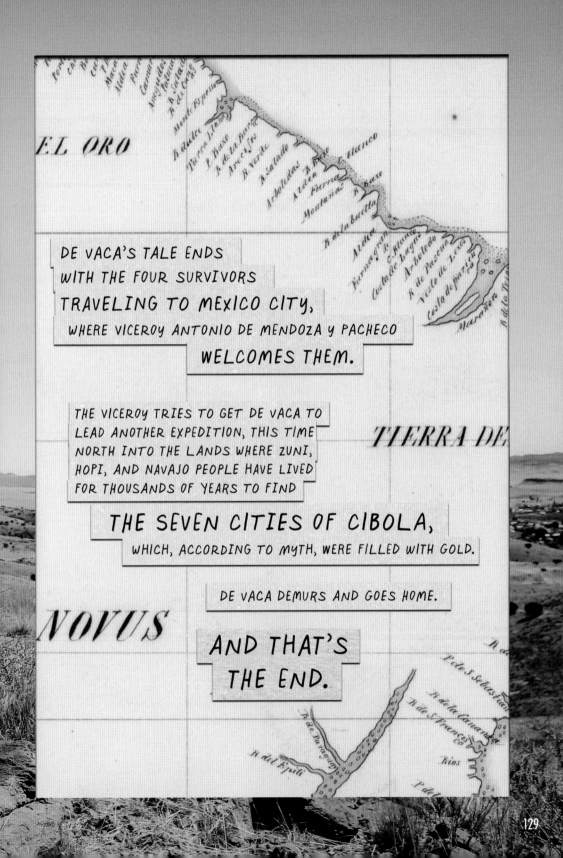

DE VACA'S TALE ENDS
WITH THE FOUR SURVIVORS
TRAVELING TO MEXICO CITY,
WHERE VICEROY ANTONIO DE MENDOZA Y PACHECO
WELCOMES THEM.

THE VICEROY TRIES TO GET DE VACA TO
LEAD ANOTHER EXPEDITION, THIS TIME
NORTH INTO THE LANDS WHERE ZUNI,
HOPI, AND NAVAJO PEOPLE HAVE LIVED
FOR THOUSANDS OF YEARS TO FIND
THE SEVEN CITIES OF CIBOLA,
WHICH, ACCORDING TO MYTH, WERE FILLED WITH GOLD.

DE VACA DEMURS AND GOES HOME.

AND THAT'S
THE END.

EXCEPT IT ISN'T.

AL-AZEMMOURI STAYS. DORANTES SELLS HIM TO THE VICEROY, WHO OFFERS HIM AS A GUIDE TO FRAY MARCOS DI NIZA, AND SENDS BOTH
TO SEARCH FOR CIBOLA.

AL-AZEMMOURI, AS ALWAYS, GOES FIRST.

HE HEADS NORTH WITH REPORTEDLY HUNDREDS OF INDIGENOUS ALLIES, TWO LARGE GREYHOUNDS, A MAGICAL, FEATHERED MEDICINAL GOURD, AND TURQUOISE PLATES MADE ESPECIALLY FOR HIS MEALS.

HE WALKS WEEKS AHEAD OF DI NIZA— ALONG THE PACIFIC COAST OF MEXICO, THROUGH TOHONO O'ODHAM AND PIMA LANDS, UP AND UP TOWARD CIBOLA.

TO KEEP IN TOUCH WITH DI NIZA, HE SENDS BACK A SERIES **OF CROSSES** (AS INSTRUCTED)— THE BIGGER THE CROSS, THE BETTER **THE RICHES** HE IS UNCOVERING.

DE NIZA KEEPS GETTING CROSSES DELIVERED. BIGGER AND BIGGER AND BIGGER UNTIL THEY ARE THE SIZE OF MEN.

AND THEN, THEY STOP.

WORD ARRIVES THAT AL-AZEMMOURI MADE IT TO HAWIKUH,
ONE OF THE SEVEN CITIES OF CIBOLA.

WORD ARRIVES THAT AL-AZEMMOURI IS DEAD.

DE NIZA NEVER SEES AL-AZEMMOURI'S BODY, AND MOST LIKELY NEVER MAKES
IT TO CIBOLA, BUT STILL REPORTEDLY RAVES ABOUT THE RICHES TO BE HAD.

FRANCISCO DE CORONADO AND HIS ARMY RETURN THE
FOLLOWING YEAR TO FIND ZUNI CITIES WITH BUILDINGS AND PEOPLE
AND RICH TRADE AND FARMS, BUT NO GOLD.

FOR AL-AZEMMOURI, HIS STORY HAS BEEN WRITTEN AGAIN AND AGAIN . . .

IN ONE VERSION HE'S KILLED BY ZUNI CHIEFS.

IN ONE HE FAKES HIS OWN DEATH WITH THE
HELP OF INDIGENOUS FRIENDS TO
ESCAPE BONDAGE.

SO MUCH IS UNKNOWN ABOUT
AL-AZEMMOURI'S LIFE AND DEATH.

WHAT IS KNOWN IS THAT TIME AND AGAIN,
AL-AZEMMOURI WENT FIRST.

A MULTILINGUAL, MUSLIM, INVOLUNTARY
INVADER, TRAVERSING MULTIPLE CULTURES
AND RELIGIONS, HE WAS THE PORTAL
BETWEEN WORLDS.

THE ONE WHO COULD BEST EXIST WITHIN THE
STRANGE LIMINAL SPACE
OF FIRST CONTACT.

THIS LAND IS YOUR LAND

"WE MUST PROTECT AND DEFEND OUR LANDS AND PEOPLES AT ALL COSTS. WE HAVE NO OTHER CHOICE."

—NATIONAL INDIAN YOUTH COUNCIL

Sorry... NO GAS

IN THE FALL OF 1973, "SORRY" SIGNS SPRANG UP
AT GAS STATIONS AROUND THE COUNTRY.

GAS WAS SUDDENLY SCARCE AND EXPENSIVE BECAUSE MIDDLE EASTERN
NATIONS HAD IMPOSED AN OIL EMBARGO AGAINST COUNTRIES ALLIED WITH
ISRAEL DURING THE YOM KIPPUR WAR. THE U.S.—INCREASINGLY DEPENDENT
ON FOREIGN OIL AND A MAJOR ISRAEL BACKER—WAS HIT HARD.

TO REDUCE ENERGY CONSUMPTION, PRESIDENT NIXON BANNED OUTDOOR CHRISTMAS
LIGHTS FOR THE SEASON, BUT IT WAS OBVIOUS FEWER LIGHT-UP SANTAS WEREN'T
GOING TO CUT IT LONG-TERM. SO THE NIXON ADMINISTRATION COMMITTED TO
RAMPING UP DOMESTIC ENERGY PRODUCTION AS
A STEP TOWARD ENERGY INDEPENDENCE.

OIL AND OTHER ENERGY SOURCES LIKE GAS AND
COAL AND URANIUM AREN'T PRODUCED, THOUGH:
THEY'RE EXTRACTED.

THE U.S. COULDN'T JUST MAKE MORE;
IT HAD TO FIND NEW SOURCES AND
NEW WAYS TO PUMP, SCRAPE,
AND HAUL THE FUELS
OUT OF THE EARTH.

THAT EXTRACTION TAKES A TOLL.

MINING AND DRILLING ARE DIRTY, DANGEROUS,
DESTRUCTIVE ENDEAVORS THAT IRREPARABLY SCAR
THE LANDSCAPE, LEACH WASTE, POISON WATER,
AND RADICALLY TRANSFORM NEARBY COMMUNITIES.

ONE OF NIXON'S SOLUTIONS FOR MEETING THE DOMESTIC
ENERGY DEMAND WAS TO DESIGNATE THE FOUR CORNERS REGION—
WHERE COLORADO, UTAH, NEW MEXICO, AND ARIZONA MEET,
AND WHERE THE DINÉ (NAVAJO), HOPI, UTE, AND ZUNI
HAVE LIVED FOR THOUSANDS OF YEARS—

A "NATIONAL SACRIFICE ZONE."

MEANING, IT WAS CLEAR THE EXTRACTION WOULD CAUSE HARM,
BUT IT WAS A PEOPLE AND A LAND
THE GOVERNMENT WAS WILLING TO SACRIFICE
FOR THE NEEDS OF THE NATION.

ALTHOUGH THERE WAS A LONG HISTORY OF OUTSIDERS CLAIMING DINÉ LAND AND EXTRACTING DINÉ RESOURCES AND LABOR—FROM SPANISH CONQUISTADORES IN THE 1600S TO MEXICAN SOLDIERS AND THE U.S. MILITARY IN THE 1800S—

AT THE TURN OF THE 20TH CENTURY, THE DINÉ REMAINED RESILIENT AND SELF-SUFFICIENT.

THEY RETAINED THEIR TRADITIONAL DECENTRALIZED
CONSENSUS-DRIVEN GOVERNMENT,
AS WELL AS THEIR CULTURE AND RELIGION
(DESPITE REPEATED U.S. ATTEMPTS AT
ETHNIC CLEANSING FROM THE LONG WALK
TO INDIAN BOARDING SCHOOLS).

THEY SUSTAINED THEMSELVES VIA
LIVESTOCK AND FARMING,
LIKE SHEEPHERDING,
AND THROUGH ARTISAN TRADE—
THE DINÉ WERE KNOWN FOR THEIR
EXPERT SILVERSMITHING
AND WEAVING ABILITIES.

AND WHEN THE 1868 TREATY OF BOSQUE REDONDO
RETURNED ONLY A SMALL PORTION OF THEIR LANDS,
THE DINÉ PERSISTED IN RECLAIMING THEIR HOMELANDS,
BUILDING THE NAVAJO NATION INTO THE
LARGEST RESERVATION IN THE COUNTRY.

ALL OF THAT BEGAN TO CHANGE IN THE 1920S, WHEN OIL SPECULATORS CAME TO NAVAJOLAND SEEKING PETROLEUM DEPOSITS THAT COULD FUEL THE BUDDING AUTO INDUSTRY.

WHEN OIL WAS DISCOVERED, AMERICAN OIL COMPANIES NEEDED A GOVERNMENTAL PARTNER THAT WOULD SIGN OIL LEASES TO THE LAND, SO THEY WORKED TO UPEND THE NAVAJO'S TRADITIONAL SYSTEM OF GOVERNMENT. THEIR INFLUENCE LED TO THE FORMATION OF THE NAVAJO NATION TRIBAL GOVERNMENT, WHICH RUBBER-STAMPED THE DEALS.

IN THE 1930S, THE U.S. GOVERNMENT DEMANDED HALF OF ALL DINÉ SHEEP, GOATS, HORSES, AND COWS—

AN ESTIMATED 500,000 ANIMALS—

BE ROUNDED UP AND SLAUGHTERED EN MASSE TO CLEAR ROOM FOR THE HYDROELECTRIC HOOVER DAM.

THE LOSS WAS BOTH ECONOMICALLY AND CULTURALLY TRAUMATIC.

NOT ONLY WERE THE DINÉ NOT COMPENSATED FOR THE LOSS, THEY WERE FORCED TO FIND OTHER WAYS TO SUPPORT THEMSELVES OFTEN BY EITHER LEAVING THEIR LANDS OR TAKING JOBS IN EXTRACTIVE INDUSTRIES.

IN THE 1940S, FIFTY YEARS OF URANIUM MINING AND MILLING WAS KICKED OFF WITH AMERICA'S QUEST TO BUILD AN ATOMIC BOMB, PULLING 3,000 DINÉ WORKERS INTO 2,500 MINES IN AND AROUND THE NAVAJO RESERVATION.

THE MINES BROUGHT INCOME, BUT THEY ALSO BROUGHT BOOMTOWN VIOLENCE; POISONED WORKERS, ANIMALS, AND WATER; AND DESECRATED HOLY SITES.

IN THE 1950S AND 1960S, MASSIVE CORPORATIONS LIKE UTAH INTERNATIONAL AND PEABODY WESTERN COAL COMPANY BEGAN EXPLORING, AND THEN INTENSIVELY MINING, THE LARGEST COAL DEPOSIT IN THE U.S. ON DINÉ AND HOPI LANDS.

ACROSS THE U.S., INDIGENOUS COMMUNITIES **HAVE BEEN DISPROPORTIONATELY** AFFECTED BY EXTRACTIVE INDUSTRIES.

NATIVE LANDS HAVE BEEN RAVAGED— IN THE U.S. NEARLY A QUARTER OF SUPERFUND SITES ARE ON INDIAN LANDS—WHILE NATIVE PEOPLE USUALLY DON'T BENEFIT FROM THE CHEAPER ENERGY THEY ARE HELPING TO CREATE.

KNOWN AS **"ENERGY INJUSTICE,"** THE PHENOMENON HAS ALSO BEEN CALLED

"RADIOACTIVE COLONIALISM"

BY WINONA LADUKE, AN OJIBWE ECONOMIST AND ENVIRONMENTALIST, WHICH SHE DEFINES AS A TANGLED RELATIONSHIP THAT HAS RESHAPED TRIBAL NATIONS' GOVERNMENTS, ECONOMIES, LANDS, AND CULTURES OVER THE PAST CENTURY.

IN 1961,

INDIGENOUS COLLEGE KIDS AND RECENT GRADS AROUND THE COUNTRY FORMED **THE NATIONAL INDIAN YOUTH COUNCIL (NIYC)** TO ENGAGE IN DIRECT ACTION AND AGITATE FOR NATIVE AMERICAN CIVIL RIGHTS.

THE GROUP ADVOCATED FOR WHAT ENCROACHING AMERICAN INDUSTRY, GOVERNMENT, AND MILITARY WERE **ERODING—** TRIBAL SOVEREIGNTY, SELF-DETERMINATION, TRADITIONAL CULTURE.

IN THE 1970S, AS RESOURCE EXPLOITATION ON INDIGENOUS LANDS RAMPED UP, THE NIYC TURNED THEIR FOCUS TO **ENVIRONMENTAL JUSTICE.**

IN 1971, TWO MASSIVE COMPANIES—UTAH INTERNATIONAL AND THE WESTERN COAL GASIFICATION COMPANY—ANNOUNCED PLANS TO LAUNCH A JOINT GASIFICATION VENTURE ON NAVAJO LANDS.

GASIFICATION—THE PROCESS THAT CONVERTS A FUEL (LIKE COAL) INTO A GAS THAT CAN THEN BE USED FOR ELECTRICITY OR GASOLINE—DEMANDS A MASSIVE AMOUNT OF WATER.

THE PROPOSED PLANTS WERE EXPECTED TO USE UP TO

32.5 BILLION GALLONS OF WATER PER YEAR AND 6 MILLION TONS OF COAL PER PLANT TO RUN.

NIYC RALLIED TO STOP THEM FROM BEING BUILT.

NATIVE YOUTH CANVASSED LOCALLY AND HELD TEACH-INS TO EDUCATE THE PUBLIC ABOUT HOW THE PLANTS WOULD **NEGATIVELY AFFECT THE ENVIRONMENT AND THE COMMUNITY,** THEY WROTE LETTERS TO THE NATIONAL PRESS TO RAISE AWARENESS ABOUT THE ISSUE, AND MADE THEIR VOICES HEARD IN WASHINGTON— PETITIONING THE SECRETARY OF THE INTERIOR— AND AT HOME— ORGANIZING A SIT-IN AT THE NAVAJO TRIBAL GOVERNMENT.

AND THEY **WON.**

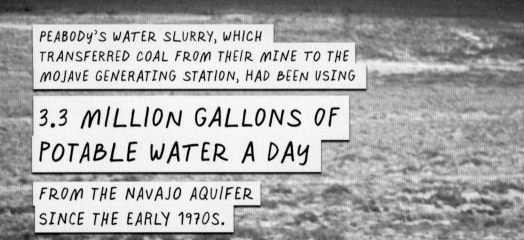

IN 2001, A NEW GENERATION OF HOPI AND DINÉ YOUTH ACTIVISTS CAME TOGETHER TO FORM THE BLACK MESA WATER COALITION (BMWC) TO FIGHT EXTRACTION AND PROTECT THEIR COMMUNITY'S WATER SUPPLY.

ALTHOUGH NIYC HAD BLOCKED THE GASIFICATION VENTURE, OTHER COMPANIES, LIKE PEABODY, HAD KEPT UP THEIR EXTRACTION EFFORTS.

PEABODY'S WATER SLURRY, WHICH TRANSFERRED COAL FROM THEIR MINE TO THE MOJAVE GENERATING STATION, HAD BEEN USING

3.3 MILLION GALLONS OF POTABLE WATER A DAY

FROM THE NAVAJO AQUIFER SINCE THE EARLY 1970S.

LIKE NIYC, BMWC SET OUT ON A LOCAL CONSCIOUSNESS-RAISING
CAMPAIGN, EDUCATING THE COMMUNITY AROUND PEABODY—
THE MAJORITY OF WHOM DIDN'T HAVE ACCESS
TO RUNNING WATER OR ELECTRICITY—
ABOUT THE COMPANY'S WATER USAGE, AND ADVOCATING
FOR MORE SUSTAINABLE ALTERNATIVES.

DUE IN PART TO BMWC'S ADVOCACY, PEABODY
CLOSED THE WATER SLURRY IN 2005,
THE NAVAJO NATION COUNCIL BECAME THE FIRST TRIBAL
GOVERNMENT TO APPROVE GREEN JOBS LEGISLATION IN 2009,
AND IN 2010 BMWC AND OTHERS
BLOCKED A COAL MINE EXPANSION EFFORT BY PEABODY.

TODAY, THE ENERGY LANDSCAPE IS CHANGING,
AND THE NAVAJO NATION IS CHANGING WITH IT.

THE URANIUM AND COAL INDUSTRIES THERE
HAVE LARGELY COLLAPSED, LEAVING BEHIND

ZOMBIE MINES—

MINES THAT ARE NO LONGER OPERATIVE,
BUT ALSO AREN'T TECHNICALLY "CLOSED"
SO THAT THEIR OWNERS DON'T NEED TO DEAL
WITH COSTLY ENVIRONMENTAL CLEANUP—

AND A NEARLY 50 PERCENT

UNEMPLOYMENT RATE.

STILL, THE OPPORTUNITY TO TRANSITION
AWAY FROM EXTRACTIVE INDUSTRIES
MAKES MANY HOPEFUL.

IN DECEMBER 2020, WAHLEAH JOHNS, FORMERLY THE EXECUTIVE DIRECTOR
OF THE BMWC, TWEETED A VIDEO OF THE NAVAJO GENERATING STACKS
BEING DEMOLISHED, SAYING,

"IT'S A STEP TOWARDS CREATING AN ENERGY SYSTEM THAT IS ALIGNED WITH OUR VALUES AS ORIGINAL CARETAKERS OF THIS LAND."

JOHNS IS ALSO THE COFOUNDER OF NATIVE RENEWABLES, AN INDIGENOUS,
WOMEN-LED COMPANY WITH THE MISSION OF EMPOWERING NATIVE AMERICAN
FAMILIES TO "ACHIEVE ENERGY INDEPENDENCE BY GROWING RENEWABLE
ENERGY CAPACITY AND AFFORDABLE ACCESS TO OFF-GRID POWER."

THEIR FIRST PROJECT WAS TO DELIVER
SOLAR TRAILERS BUILT BY NAVAJO ENGINEERS
TO HELP POWER THE GROWING CAMP AT STANDING ROCK—
ANOTHER INDIGENOUS ACTIVIST EFFORT TO PROTECT
A REGION'S WATER FROM ENERGY COMPANIES—IN 2016.

THE COMPANY IS CURRENTLY WORKING TO PROVIDE
OFF-GRID SOLAR POWER TO 15,000 NAVAJO HOUSEHOLDS.

147

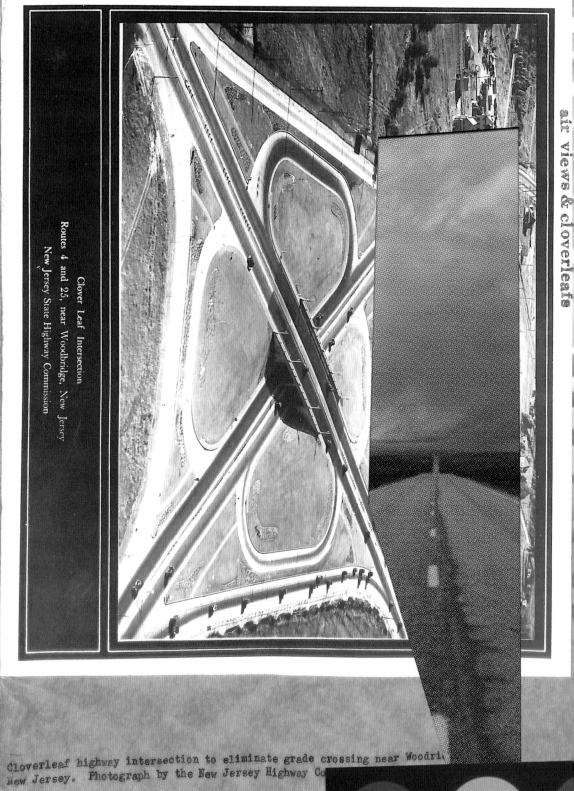

Clover Leaf Intersection
Routes 4 and 25, near Woodbridge, New Jersey
New Jersey State Highway Commission

Cloverleaf highway intersection to eliminate grade crossing near Woodri...
New Jersey. Photograph by the New Jersey Highway Co...

A CAR IN EVERY GARAGE

"THERE'S A FREEWAY RUNNIN' THROUGH THE YARD"

—LYRICS FROM TOM PETTY'S "FREE FALLIN'"

IT'S HARD TO IMAGINE
AN AMERICA WITH NO CARS.

NO DRIVE-THRUS OR ROAD TRIPS.

NO PARKING LOTS OR GAS STATIONS.

NO SUBURBAN SPRAWL OR ENDLESS MALLS.

AND NO FREEWAYS.

AT THE TURN OF THE 20TH CENTURY, PEOPLE GOT AROUND CITIES BY WALKING, BICYCLING, RIDING HORSES, TAKING STREETCARS, PULLING WAGONS, RIDING TRAINS, AND PACKING INTO SUBWAYS.

STREETS WERE SHARED BY EVERYONE—

A PEDESTRIAN HAD JUST AS MUCH A RIGHT TO THE ROAD AS A BREAD CART.

EARLY AUTOMOTIVE MANUFACTURERS AND BOOSTERS—LIKE OIL CORPORATIONS AND WEALTHY AUTOMOBILE ENTHUSIASTS—REALIZED THAT IN ORDER FOR CARS TO TAKE HOLD, THEY NEEDED TO TRANSFORM THE BUILT ENVIRONMENT, LAWS, AND PUBLIC OPINION TO FAVOR CARS.

OVER THE COURSE OF THE EARLY TO MID-20TH CENTURY, LAND-USE LAW, CRIMINAL LAW, INSURANCE, VEHICLE SAFETY REGULATIONS, AND EVEN THE TAX CODE **WERE ALL SHAPED TO INCENTIVIZE AUTOMOBILE USE.**

CARS WERE PORTRAYED AS CONVENIENT, EFFICIENT, FUTURISTIC.

UNLIKE PUBLIC TRANSPORTATION, WHERE EVERYONE SAT TOGETHER, CARS WERE PRIVATE, ALLOWING DRIVERS TO GO WHEREVER THEY WANTED, WHENEVER THEY WANTED, WITH EXACTLY WHO THEY WANTED.

POST WORLD WAR II, THE SUBURBS SWELLED AND COMMUTES INCREASED. SO DID TRAFFIC.

IN 1956, PRESIDENT EISENHOWER SIGNED THE NATIONAL INTERSTATE AND DEFENSE HIGHWAYS ACT, A MASSIVE PUBLIC-WORKS PROJECT THAT AUTHORIZED $51 BILLION TO BE SPENT IN UNDER TWENTY YEARS ON THE BUILDING OF TENS OF THOUSANDS **OF MILES OF NEW FREEWAYS** TO MAKE SUBURBAN COMMUTES MORE EFFICIENT, AND TO CONNECT RURAL AND URBAN AMERICA.

THE FEDERAL GOVERNMENT OFFERED TO COVER **90 PERCENT** OF THE COST OF BUILDING THE NEW FREEWAYS.

FOR CITY PLANNERS IN THE 1950S LOOKING TO CONNECT THEIR DOWNTOWNS WITH THE NEW SUBURBS, THE OFFER **WAS IRRESISTIBLE.**

THE NEW MULTI-LANE EXPRESSWAY
PROJECTS WERE IMMENSE,
AND CITIES DIDN'T JUST HAVE
LOTS OF LAND LYING AROUND.
PLANNERS AND OFFICIALS LOOKED AT MAPS
TO DECIDE WHAT TO DEMOLISH, AND SAW IT
AS THE PERFECT OPPORTUNITY FOR

"URBAN RENEWAL."

THEY SOUGHT OUT PLACES WHERE LAND WAS CHEAP
AND ANY OPPOSITION COULD BE EASILY QUELLED.
BECAUSE OF DECADES OF REDLINING—THE
SYSTEMATIC PRACTICE OF DENYING BLACK
HOMEOWNERS ACCESS TO MORTGAGES IN WHITER
AREAS OF THE CITY, AND THE SUBSEQUENT
REFUSAL TO INVEST IN BLACK NEIGHBORHOODS—
LAND WAS MUCH CHEAPER IF
WHITE PEOPLE DIDN'T LIVE ON IT.

AND BECAUSE OF THE DISPROPORTIONATELY WHITE LEADERSHIP
IN BOTH LOCAL GOVERNMENTS AND COMMERCIAL INTERESTS,
POLITICAL INFLUENCE WAS SIGNIFICANTLY WEAKER IN THOSE
NEIGHBORHOODS AS WELL.

EVEN WITH THE MASSIVE POWER IMBALANCES,
LOCAL COMMUNITIES WHOSE NEIGHBORHOODS
WERE SLATED FOR DEMOLITION PUSHED BACK.

IN THE FEW CASES WHERE HIGHWAYS WERE PROPOSED TO RUN THROUGH
WHITER AND WEALTHIER COMMUNITIES, ADVOCATES USUALLY FORCED
ROUTES TO CHANGE, LIKE JANE JACOBS'S FAMOUS SHOWDOWN WITH
ROBERT MOSES THAT BLOCKED THE I-78 FROM BEING BUILT THROUGH
THE WEST VILLAGE IN NEW YORK CITY.

Roduce to 4"

SOME ADVOCATES IN NONWHITE NEIGHBORHOODS
WERE ALSO SUCCESSFUL, SUCH AS SAMMIE ABDULLAH
ABBOTT AND REGINALD H. BOOKER, WHO FORMED THE
EMERGENCY COALITION ON THE TRANSPORTATION CRISIS
TO BLOCK A SERIES OF PLANNED BELTWAYS IN
WASHINGTON, DC.

THEIR SLOGAN—"WHITE MEN'S ROADS
THROUGH BLACK MEN'S HOMES"—

RALLIED PROTESTORS TO SUSTAINED ACTIONS
THAT ADVOCATED FOR INVESTMENT IN THE
WASHINGTON METRO SYSTEM INSTEAD.

MANY BLACK, BROWN, AND IMMIGRANT COMMUNITIES, HOWEVER, LACKED THE **POLITICAL AND ECONOMIC** CAPITAL TO FULLY BLOCK THE PROPOSED FREEWAYS.

THEY WON WHERE THEY COULD—LIKE FIGHTING FOR BELOW-GRADE CONSTRUCTION, SO THAT EVEN IF A ROAD TORE THEIR NEIGHBORHOOD IN TWO, AT LEAST THE FREEWAY WASN'T TOWERING OVER THEM.

ACROSS THE COUNTRY, NEIGHBORHOODS WERE RAZED AND REMADE.

FROM DETROIT'S **BLACK BOTTOM AND PARADISE VALLEY**

TO MIAMI'S **OVERTOWN**

TO **THE RONDO** IN ST. PAUL/MINNEAPOLIS

TO **TREMÉ** IN NEW ORLEANS,

PREDOMINANTLY BLACK NEIGHBORHOODS **WERE TORN APART.**

BLACK-OWNED BUSINESSES AND HOMES WERE DEMOLISHED, TREE-LINED BOULEVARDS AND PUBLIC SPACES WERE PAVED OVER, AND HUNDREDS UPON HUNDREDS OF BLACK FAMILIES WERE DISPLACED.

SUGAR HILL IN LOS ANGELES,

HAMLIN PARK IN BUFFALO,

THE HISTORIC WESTSIDE IN LAS VEGAS,

WEST END IN CINCINNATI,

BEL AIR IN MONTGOMERY,

15TH WARD IN SYRACUSE,

ELYRIA IN DENVER,

IN THE 1950S, '60S, AND EARLY '70S, CITY AFTER CITY **WAS SLICED UP AND HOLLOWED OUT.**

FOR

Structures — Grade Separations
Air Views & Clover Leafs   56-261

California

THOSE WHO STAYED WERE LEFT WITH

SHELLS OF THEIR FORMER COMMUNITIES,

CUT OFF FROM OTHER PARTS OF THEIR CITY,
ENGULFED BY CONSTANT CAR TRAFFIC.

THE POLLUTION SURROUNDING FREEWAYS IS INCREDIBLY TOXIC.

IT CAN DRIFT FOR A MILE OR MORE,
BUT POOLS IN ESPECIALLY HIGH-RISK ZONES
500 TO 1,000 FEET FROM THE ROADS.

VEHICLE POLLUTION IS PROVEN TO CAUSE HIGHER
RATES OF ASTHMA, CANCER, HEART ATTACK,
STROKE, RESPIRATORY COMPLICATIONS, AND
PRE-TERM BIRTHS, AS WELL AS PUT PEOPLE AT
HIGHER RISK FOR DEMENTIA.

TODAY, CARS AND TRUCKS ACCOUNT
FOR ALMOST ONE-FIFTH OF ALL U.S.
CARBON EMISSIONS—A MAJOR SOURCE
OF CLIMATE CHANGE.

AS THE FREEWAYS BUILT IN THE MID-20TH CENTURY AGE AND DEMAND REPAIR, COMMUNITY GROUPS ACROSS THE COUNTRY ARE ENCOURAGING CITIES TO RECONSIDER WHAT THE FUTURE MIGHT LOOK LIKE IF THEY

ABANDONED FREEWAYS AND INVESTED IN PEOPLE OVER CARS—

CLEANER AIR, WATERFRONT ACCESS, TREE-LINED BOULEVARDS, BIKE PATHS, PEDESTRIAN-FOCUSED SHOPPING DISTRICTS, MORE EQUITABLE TRANSPORTATION SOLUTIONS.

MANY CITIES HAVE HEARD THE CALL AND ARE IN THE PROCESS OF DEMOLISHING OR REPLACING THEIR HIGHWAYS, BUT OTHER CITIES, LIKE PORTLAND, OREGON, ARE STILL FOCUSED ON EXPANSION.

A GROUP OF TEEN CLIMATE ACTIVISTS
KNOWN AS "YOUTH VS. ODOT"

STARTED PROTESTING THE OREGON DEPARTMENT OF TRANSPORTATION IN 2021 WITH THE INTENT OF EXPLICITLY TYING FREEWAY EXPANSION TO CLIMATE CHANGE IN THE PUBLIC'S MIND.

THE GROUP HAS LINKED UP WITH OTHER NATIONAL CLIMATE ORGS LIKE SUNRISE MOVEMENT, AND LOCAL TRANSPORTATION AND RACIAL JUSTICE ACTIVISTS, TO STOP THE CITY FROM REPEATING PAST INJUSTICES—LIKE SPENDING OVER A BILLION DOLLARS TO WIDEN A STRETCH OF THE FREEWAY THAT RUNS THROUGH ALBINA, A HISTORICALLY BLACK NEIGHBORHOOD.

THE FIGHT MAY TAKE YEARS, BUT YOUTH ACTIVISTS ARE IN IT FOR THE LONG HAUL, ABLE TO ENVISION A WORLD LESS DEPENDENT ON CARS IN A WAY THAT MANY ADULTS CANNOT.

WHITE
PICKET FENCES

"LIVE BETTER IN A HOME OF YOUR OWN"

—SLOGAN FROM A MID-CENTURY ADVERTISEMENT FOR A SUBURBAN HOUSE

IN THE LATE 19TH AND EARLY 20TH CENTURIES, HOUSING WAS MUCH MORE FLEXIBLE, FLUID, AND COMMUNAL THAN IT IS TODAY— ESPECIALLY IN AMERICA'S BOOMING CITIES.

THE RAPIDLY GROWING DOWNTOWNS NEEDED PEOPLE, SO MANY PEOPLE, TO FUEL THEM:

DAY LABORERS

SEAFARERS

MIGRANT WORKERS

FACTORY WORKERS

NEWLY MINTED WOMEN WORKERS

AND EVERY WORKER, NO MATTER HOW INDUSTRIOUS, HAD TO SLEEP SOMEWHERE.

THE BED WAS THE MOST BASIC UNIT OF HOUSING, AND WORKERS HAD THE ABILITY TO RENT ONE IN ANY WAY THEY NEEDED.

THERE WERE "HOT BEDS" RENTED IN SHIFTS, BEDS IN SHARED ROOMS, BEDS IN PRIVATE ROOMS WITH SHARED BATHROOMS, BEDS WITH PRIVATE BATHROOMS AND SHARED KITCHENS. WORKERS LIVED IN HOTELS, BOARDED IN PRIVATE HOMES, RENTED BEDS BY THE NIGHT, THE WEEK, THE MONTH, THE SEASON.

AT THE TURN OF THE CENTURY,
SAN FRANCISCO WAS KNOWN AS

HOTEL CITY

BECAUSE VAST NUMBERS OF PEOPLE

LIVED IN HOTELS

AND ATE ONLY IN RESTAURANTS.

IN NEW YORK, AN 1892 GUIDE TO THE CITY
CLAIMED THAT WHEN IT CAME TO HOUSING,
"EVERY INDIVIDUAL CAPRICE AND PURSE
CAN FIND SOMETHING TO SUIT."

BOSTON'S SOUTH END ROOMING
HOUSES WERE KNOWN TO SHELTER
EVERYONE FROM CLERKS TO
PAINTERS, SHOP GIRLS TO
ELECTRICIANS, BLACK
RAILROAD PORTERS TO
POLICEMEN, NURSES TO
CARPENTERS.

CHICAGO HAD DISTRICTS
KNOWN FOR DIFFERENT TYPES
OF RESIDENTIAL HOTELS:
ROOMING HOUSES ON THE
NORTH SIDE, AND CHEAP
LODGING HOUSES NEAR
THE MAIN STEM.

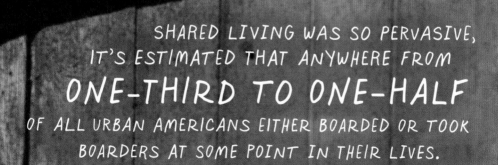

OOMS
Y and NIGHT
MINNIE

SHARED LIVING WAS SO PERVASIVE,
IT'S ESTIMATED THAT ANYWHERE FROM
ONE-THIRD TO ONE-HALF
OF ALL URBAN AMERICANS EITHER BOARDED OR TOOK
BOARDERS AT SOME POINT IN THEIR LIVES.

WHERE YOU SLEPT WAS OF COURSE DEFINED BY WHAT YOU COULD PAY (AS WELL AS YOUR SKIN COLOR AND COUNTRY OF BIRTH), CONFERRING SOCIAL STATUS AND DEFINING SOCIAL LIFE.

JUST AS NEW YORK CITY'S BARBIZON PROVIDED AN EXCLUSIVE PLATFORM FOR AMBITIOUS WEALTHY WHITE WOMEN, THE INTERNATIONAL HOTEL IN SAN FRANCISCO PROVIDED AN AFFORDABLE HAVEN AND SHARED CULTURE FOR FILIPINO FAMILIES, AND THE CHICAGO BEACH HOTEL PROVIDED ITS MAJORITY JEWISH RESIDENTS A CHANCE TO SOCIALLY MIX WITH GENTILES.

THE BED AS THE PRIMARY UNIT OF HOUSING MEANT
HOUSEWIVES RENTING OUT ROOMS
OFTEN HAD MORE RELIABLE INCOME
THAN THEIR HUSBANDS,

SINGLE WORKERS (ESPECIALLY WOMEN)
COULD WORK WITHOUT THE CRUSHING
BURDEN OF HOUSEWORK,

THE GREAT DEPRESSION'S
NEWLY POOR
COULD KEEP A ROOF OVER THEIR
HEADS AS THEY TRIED TO CLAW
THEIR WAY BACK UP,

AND EVERYONE WHO WANTED
COULD PAY FOR JUST AS MUCH

"HOME"

AS THEY NEEDED.

IN THE 1930S, THE TERM "SRO"—
SINGLE-ROOM OCCUPANCY—
CAME TO DEFINE ALL TYPES OF
FLEXIBLE HOUSING.

THROUGHOUT WORLD WAR II,
WARTIME WORKERS FLOWED INTO SROS,
AND WHEN THEY EBBED OUT,
WOUNDED SOLDIERS
WASHED IN.

AND WHEN THE ELDERLY,
THE DISABLED, AND
THE MENTALLY ILL
WERE BOOTED OUT
OF ASYLUMS AND
INSTITUTIONS AS
THEY SHUT DOWN,
THESE PEOPLE TOO
SOUGHT OUT THEIR
SINGLE ROOMS.

BY THE 1950S, THERE
WERE 200,000 SROS
IN NYC—OVER 10 PERCENT OF THE
CITY'S RENTAL STOCK AT THE TIME.

POST-WORLD WAR II, NUCLEAR FAMILIES LIVING IN
SPACIOUS SINGLE-FAMILY HOMES
BECAME THE POSTCARD IMAGE OF THE AMERICAN DREAM.

THERE WAS INCREASINGLY LITTLE ACCEPTANCE
FOR A PLACE WHERE ALL KINDS OF PEOPLE WOULD
STREAM IN AND OUT, ROOM BY ROOM, BED BY BED.

MIDDLE-CLASS
WHITE PEOPLE
FLED TO
THE MAJORITY-
WHITE SUBURBS,

AND URBAN SROS WERE BRANDED AS POOR-PEOPLE
HOUSING, BECOMING A SYMBOL FOR ALL THE
SOCIETAL ILLS POVERTY BEGETS—VIOLENCE,
INSTABILITY, UNSAFE LIVING CONDITIONS—
AND CITIES SOUGHT TO ELIMINATE THEM.

IN 1955, NYC **BANNED CONSTRUCTION** OF SROS, AND MADE IT **ILLEGAL** TO CHOP UP HOUSES INTO SMALLER UNITS.

BY THE MID- TO **LATE-1970S,** SROS WERE BEING **DEMONIZED IN THE PRESS** AS FRIGHTFUL MURDEROUS PLACES, AND THE CITY GAVE **LANDLORDS TAX BREAKS** TO CONVERT SROS TO HIGHER-PRICED APARTMENTS.

AT THE SAME TIME, SAN FRANCISCO WAS **BATTLING PROTESTORS** PROTECTING LONG-TERM SRO RESIDENTS.

BETWEEN THE MID-1970S AND THE 1990S, **ONE MILLION SRO UNITS** WERE DESTROYED.

DENVER **LOST NEARLY 2/3** OF ITS UNITS

CHICAGO **LOST 80%** OF ITS UNITS BETWEEN 1960-1980

NYC **LOST 60%** OF ITS UNITS BETWEEN 1975-1981

SEATTLE LOST **15,000 UNITS** BETWEEN 1960-1981

PORTLAND **LOST 1,700** UNITS

SAN DIEGO LOST 1,247 UNITS BETWEEN 1976-1984

BY THE 1980S, THE SROS THAT REMAINED WERE BEING CONVERTED INTO **LUXURY CO-OPS.**

AND INCREASINGLY, **PEOPLE BECAME UNHOUSED.**

CITIES QUICKLY REALIZED THAT THEY HAD RAZED ROOMS INTEGRAL TO THEIR RESIDENTS' SURVIVAL WITH NO BACKUP PLAN.

WHAT'S WORSE, BY UPROOTING LEGAL SROS, THE CITY SEEDED **ILLEGAL SROS.**

IN 2013, HALF A **MILLION** NEW YORKERS WERE THOUGHT TO LIVE IN POTENTIALLY DANGEROUS AND ILLEGAL SRO UNITS.

(A YEAR LATER INVESTOR INTEREST CONTINUED TO "SURGE" IN SROS BECAUSE THEY FLIPPED SO NICELY INTO CONDOS.)

THERE IS STILL SOME
TRULY SUPPORTIVE SINGLE-ROOM HOUSING,
LIKE CAPITOL HALL ON WEST 87TH STREET IN NEW YORK CITY—
AN SRO THAT WAS BOUGHT BY NEIGHBORS IN THE 1980S AND
UNDERWENT AN EXTENSIVE RENOVATION IN 2016.

ITS 200 TENANTS PAY NO MORE THAN
30 PERCENT OF THEIR INCOME ON RENT,
AND HAVE ACCESS TO WEEKLY VISITS FROM SOCIAL WORKERS
AND NURSE PRACTITIONERS.

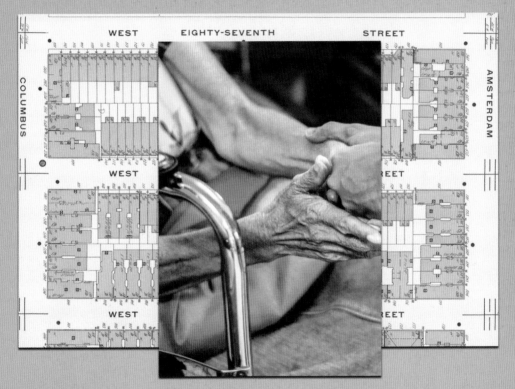

BUT EVEN THOUGH THE DAILY COST OF
OPERATING A SUPPORTIVE HOUSING UNIT IS
ONE-THIRD LESS THAN THE COST OF A SHELTER,
TWO-THIRDS LESS THAN JAIL,
AND A FRACTION OF THE COST OF A HOSPITAL,
CITIES ARE FAILING TO PROVIDE
ADEQUATE OPTIONS FOR CITIZENS WHO NEED THEM.

SO PEOPLE ARE TAKING HOUSING INTO THEIR OWN HANDS.

DURING THE COVID-19 PANDEMIC IN 2020, MOTHERS ACROSS THE COUNTRY, FROM OAKLAND TO LA TO PHILADELPHIA—DESPERATE TO FIND A WAY TO KEEP THEIR FAMILIES SAFE, TOGETHER, AND IN THEIR OWN NEIGHBORHOODS—GOT CREATIVE.

OCCUPY PHA—A GROUP OF ACTIVISTS IN PHILADELPHIA—ORGANIZED A

SIX-MONTH DIRECT-ACTION CAMPAIGN

TO FORCE THE CITY TO RESPOND TO A LACK OF SAFE, AFFORDABLE HOUSING. THEY ERECTED A PROTEST ENCAMPMENT ACROSS THE STREET FROM THE

HOUSING AUTHORITY'S HEADQUARTERS, AND BEGAN SQUATTING IN AND FIXING UP LONG-VACANT, CITY-OWNED PROPERTIES FOR FAMILIES IN NEED.

BY JULY 2020, ELEVEN FAMILIES HAD BEEN MOVED IN.

BY SEPTEMBER—AFTER MONTHS OF ACTIONS THAT INCLUDED EVERYTHING FROM BARRICADING AND BLOCKADING STREETS, TO DEFENDING THE ENCAMPMENTS—THE ACTIVISTS WON THEIR BATTLE.

THE CITY AGREED TO TRANSFER FIFTY PROPERTIES TO
A COMMUNITY LAND TRUST

FOUNDED BY PHILADELPHIA HOUSING ACTION—"A COALITION OF HOUSING ACTIVISTS WHO HAVE ALL EXPERIENCED EITHER HOMELESSNESS OR INSTITUTIONALIZATION." THE PROPERTIES ARE TO BE USED FOR EXTREMELY LOW-INCOME HOUSING AND MANAGED BY LOCAL COMMITTEES.

AS MORE AND MORE UNHOUSED AND MARGINALLY HOUSED MOTHERS ACROSS THE COUNTRY ARE FINDING SUCCESS IN THEIR DIRECT ACTIONS, THEY SAY IT'S NOT JUST ABOUT A SINGLE FAMILY, OR A SINGLE HOME.

IT'S THE BEGINNING OF A MOVEMENT

WISH YOU WERE HERE

"WHY ARE WE, AS NATIVE PEOPLE,
SUBJUGATED IN OUR OWN LAND?"

—HAUNANI-KAY TRASK

HAWAI'I IS KNOWN FOR PALM TREES AND WHITE-SAND BEACHES AND SURFERS AND SNORKLING AND SPECTACULAR, SUN-DRENCHED VISTAS.

THE ISLANDS ARE ALSO KNOWN AS HAVING ONE OF THE HIGHEST PER CAPITA RATES OF PEOPLE **EXPERIENCING HOMELESSNESS** IN THE U.S.—A CRISIS THAT DISPROPORTIONATELY AFFECTS **NATIVE HAWAIIANS.**

OF THE

HAWAIIAN ISLANDS

STATUTE MILES

NAUTICAL MILES

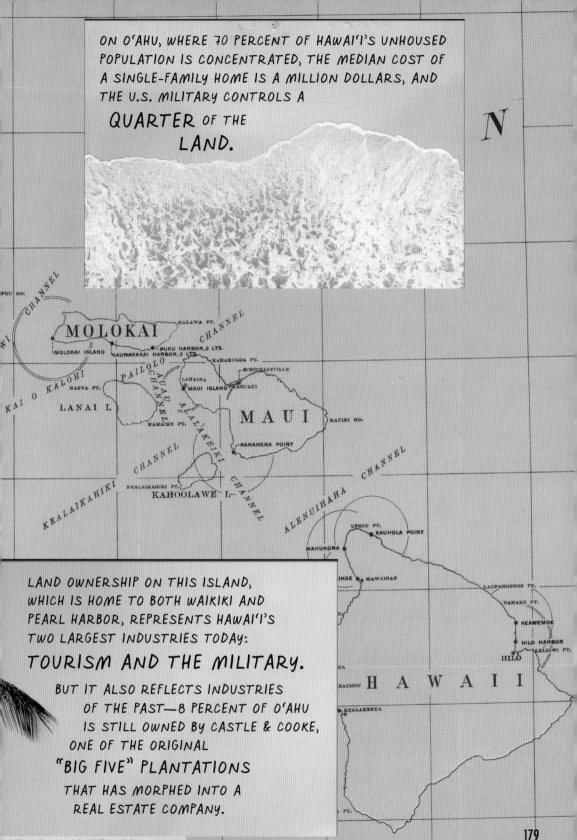

ON O'AHU, WHERE 70 PERCENT OF HAWAI'I'S UNHOUSED POPULATION IS CONCENTRATED, THE MEDIAN COST OF A SINGLE-FAMILY HOME IS A MILLION DOLLARS, AND THE U.S. MILITARY CONTROLS A QUARTER OF THE LAND.

N

LAND OWNERSHIP ON THIS ISLAND, WHICH IS HOME TO BOTH WAIKIKI AND PEARL HARBOR, REPRESENTS HAWAI'I'S TWO LARGEST INDUSTRIES TODAY: TOURISM AND THE MILITARY.

BUT IT ALSO REFLECTS INDUSTRIES OF THE PAST—8 PERCENT OF O'AHU IS STILL OWNED BY CASTLE & COOKE, ONE OF THE ORIGINAL "BIG FIVE" PLANTATIONS THAT HAS MORPHED INTO A REAL ESTATE COMPANY.

es indicate the ranges of visibility and characteristics

WHEN WHITE PROTESTANT MISSIONARIES FIRST CAME TO HAWAI'I FROM NEW ENGLAND IN 1820, THEY ENCOUNTERED A CULTURE RADICALLY DIFFERENT FROM THEIR OWN— ONE THAT PLACED AN EMPHASIS ON THE **COMMUNAL, NOT THE INDIVIDUAL,** LIVING IN RELATIONSHIP WITH NATURE, NOT CAPITAL.

THE MISSIONARIES SAW THE ISLANDERS AS "VILE" AND "COVERED WITH EVERY ABOMINATION," AND SET OUT TO "CIVILIZE" THEM INTO CHRISTIANITY.

NATIVE HAWAIIANS, REELING FROM THE MASS DEATH **DISEASED BRITISH EXPLORERS** HAD BROUGHT JUST FORTY YEARS EARLIER— THE HAWAIIAN POPULATION HAD PLUMMETED **BY 71 PERCENT** AT THAT POINT AND WAS CONTINUING TO DECLINE— WERE SUSCEPTIBLE TO PROMISES OF EVERLASTING LIFE.

IN ADDITION TO CONVERTING HAWAIIANS **TO THEIR RELIGION,** MISSIONARIES ALSO SOUGHT TO CONVERT **HAWAIIAN LANDS INTO THEIR PROPERTY.**

LAND TRANSACTIONS WERE COMPLICATED SINCE HAWAIIANS, WHO REFERRED TO THEMSELVES AS KAMAʻĀINA, OR "PEOPLE OF THE LAND," HAD LITTLE NOTION OF HOW A CASH TRANSACTION COULD DEPRIVE THEM OF THEIR HOMELANDS.

SO MISSIONARIES WORKED THEIR WAY INTO THE GOVERNMENT—BECOMING ADVISORS TO HAWAIIAN CHIEFS AND THE KING—TO CHANGE LAND OWNERSHIP CUSTOMS AND LAWS.

IN 1848, THE GREAT MĀHELE ACT DRASTICALLY TRANSFORMED HAWAIʻI'S LAND USE, ALLOWING PRIVATE LAND OWNERSHIP FOR THE FIRST TIME AND PAVING THE WAY FOR MISSIONARIES TO BECOME BUSINESS BARONS IN A PLANTATION-BASED ECONOMY.

AS THE HAWAIIAN ADAGE GOES:

"THE MISSIONARIES CAME TO DO GOOD AND STAYED TO DO WELL."

SUGAR PLANTATIONS,
BACKED BY AMERICAN CAPITAL
AND OWNED BY THE MISSIONARIES AND THEIR SONS,
BEGAN TO BE CULTIVATED ON THE ISLANDS IN THE
1850S AS A NEW SOURCE OF SUGAR FOR THE US.

UNTIL THE MID-19TH CENTURY, THE U.S. HAD IMPORTED
SUGAR FROM SLAVE-POWERED PLANTATIONS IN BOTH
THE CARIBBEAN AND THE US SOUTH. WHEN SLAVERY
WAS OUTLAWED—FIRST BY THE BRITISH EMPIRE, AND
THEN BY THE UNITED STATES—THOSE SUGAR SOURCES
WERE LOST. HAWAIIAN PLANTATIONS FILLED THE GAP,
AND THEIR SUGAR EXPORTS TO THE US BROUGHT
MASSIVE WEALTH TO WHITE PLANTERS.

THEY ALSO BROUGHT A HUGE
POPULATION SHIFT,
AS PLANTERS SHIPPED IN THOUSANDS
UPON THOUSANDS OF CONTRACT
LABORERS FROM CHINA, JAPAN, KOREA,
THE PHILIPPINES, AND PORTUGAL TO KEEP
THE PLANTATIONS RUNNING.

IN 1875, WHITE PLANTERS FURTHER SOLIDIFIED THEIR POWER
(AND AMERICAN INFLUENCE) WHEN THEY PUSHED THE KING INTO
SIGNING A "RECIPROCITY TREATY" WITH THE US THAT ALLOWED
HAWAIIAN PLANTATIONS TO EXPORT SUGAR TO THE STATES
TAX-FREE.

IN 1884, WHEN THE TREATY WAS EXTENDED, A PROVISION
WAS ADDED THAT GAVE THE US EXCLUSIVE RIGHTS TO
MILITARY BASES ON THE ISLANDS.

NATIVE HAWAIIANS WERE FURIOUS, AND PROTESTS ERUPTED.

THE KING CALLED ON HUNDREDS OF AMERICAN SOLDIERS AND MARINES TO QUELL THE UNREST, WHICH TOOK OVER A WEEK TO SUBDUE.

ANTICIPATING FURTHER RESISTANCE, ALL-WHITE SECRET SOCIETIES AND MILITIAS LIKE THE "HAWAIIAN LEAGUE" AND THE "HONOLULU RIFLES" FORMED TO PROTECT WHITE MINORITY RULE. IN 1887, THE HONOLULU RIFLES FORCED THE KING TO SIGN A NEW CONSTITUTION AT GUNPOINT.

THIS BAYONET CONSTITUTION BARRED ASIAN CONTRACT LABORERS FROM VOTING, AND INSTITUTED INCOME AND WEALTH REQUIREMENTS FOR EVERYONE ELSE, EFFECTIVELY BLOCKING MOST NATIVE HAWAIIANS FROM THE BALLOT BOX. IT ALSO LIMITED THE POWERS OF THE MONARCH, INSTEAD PUTTING GREATER POWER IN THE HANDS OF THE CABINET (WHICH, BY THAT TIME, WAS MADE UP ALMOST EXCLUSIVELY OF WHITE MEN).

BY 1890, JUST 8 PERCENT OF HAWAI'I'S POPULATION WAS WHITE, BUT THAT 8 PERCENT CONTROLLED 75 PERCENT OF HAWAI'I'S ARABLE LAND.

IN 1891, QUEEN LILI'UOKALANI TOOK THE THRONE.

SEEKING TO BOTH RESTORE POWER TO THE MONARCHY AS WELL AS RE-EMPOWER NATIVE HAWAIIANS, SHE TRAVELED THE ISLANDS AND FOUND THAT NATIVE CITIZENS WERE OVERWHELMINGLY IN SUPPORT OF CREATING A NEW CONSTITUTION.

SO SHE DRAFTED A CONSTITUTION THAT ELIMINATED PROPERTY QUALIFICATIONS FOR VOTING, AND DILUTED THE POWER OF THE WHITE ELITE.

WHEN LORRIN THURSTON, AUTHOR OF THE BAYONET CONSTITUTION AND GRANDSON OF AMERICAN MISSIONARIES, FOUND OUT ABOUT THE QUEEN'S PLAN HE WAS ENRAGED.

HE KICKED OFF A COUP,

CONVENING THE "COMMITTEE OF SAFETY"— THIRTEEN MEN, NONE OF THEM NATIVE, MOST OF THEM WITH INVESTMENTS IN PLANTATIONS AND BUSINESSES—WHICH DECLARED THAT THE COUNTRY WAS IN DANGER, THE QUEEN A THREAT, AND THAT THE SOLUTION WAS TO ANNEX HAWAI'I TO THE UNITED STATES.

HE ALSO GOT U.S. DIPLOMAT JOHN L. STEVENS ON BOARD, WHO SUMMONED HUNDREDS OF U.S. SAILORS AND MARINES TO LAND ON OʻAHU.

AND SO, ON JANUARY 17, 1893, THE UNITED STATES **OVERTHREW** THE KINGDOM OF HAWAIʻI.

THE QUEEN WAS PLACED ON HOUSE ARREST, AND SANFORD DOLE WAS NAMED PRESIDENT OF A PROVISIONAL HAWAIIAN GOVERNMENT. HE AND HIS CABINET WERE ALL WHITE, AMERICAN MEN.

THE HAWAIIAN LANGUAGE WAS BANNED IN 1896, AND IN 1898 HAWAIʻI WAS OFFICIALLY ANNEXED AS A TERRITORY OF THE UNITED STATES, TRANSFERRING NEARLY TWO MILLION ACRES OF LAND TO THE UNITED STATES GOVERNMENT IN THE PROCESS.

AFTER ANNEXATION, HAWAIIAN SUGARCANE COMPANIES BENEFITED GREATLY.

FIVE OF THEM BALLOONED INTO MULTIMILLION-DOLLAR CONGLOMERATES THAT BECAME KNOWN AS THE "BIG FIVE" DUE TO THEIR OUTSIZED POWER.

THEY CONTROLLED 90 PERCENT OF THE SUGAR BUSINESS, AND ALL HAD DESCENDANTS OF MISSIONARIES ON THEIR BOARDS OF DIRECTORS.

THE U.S. MILITARY ALSO BENEFITED GREATLY FROM ANNEXATION AND EXPANDED INTO THE CEDED LANDS, ESTABLISHING MULTIPLE BASES, LIKE PEARL HARBOR, TO FORTIFY THE ISLANDS.

IN DEVELOPING HAWAI'I INTO A STRATEGIC MILITARY ASSET, THE UNITED STATES ALSO OPENED IT UP TO BEING A PRIME LOCATION TO TARGET.

WHEN PEARL HARBOR WAS ATTACKED BY JAPAN IN 1941, HAWAI'I WAS PLACED UNDER MARTIAL LAW— INCLUDING CURFEW, COMMUNICATION CENSORSHIP, AND ARMY CONTROL OF HOSPITALS, FOOD, AND MORE—FOR THREE YEARS.

RESTRICTIONS ON JAPANESE RESIDENTS OF HAWAI'I—37 PERCENT OF THE POPULATION— WERE EVEN MORE SEVERE.

POST-WAR, STATEHOOD WAS IMPOSED ON HAWAI'I BY THE U.S. GOVERNMENT, AND HAWAI'I SHIFTED FROM A PLANTATION ECONOMY TO **A TOURISM ECONOMY.**

AMERICANS **COMMODIFIED** HAWAIIAN CULTURE AND SOLD IT FOR THE PROFIT AND ENTERTAINMENT OF NON-NATIVES— THE WORD "ALOHA," LEIS, THE HULA, LUAUS.

A 1966 ARTICLE ENTITLED "WHERE ARISTOCRATS DO THE HULA AND VOTE REPUBLICAN" SHOWS FOURTH AND FIFTH GENERATION DESCENDANTS OF MISSIONARIES RESTORING **THEIR PALATIAL ESTATES,** SITTING ON EACH OTHER'S BOARDS, TALKING ABOUT GOING BAREFOOT, MAKING THEIR OWN LEIS, AND EATING TRADITIONAL HAWAIIAN FOODS.

TOURISM EXPLODED,

ESPECIALLY AMONG WHITE AMERICANS,

LEADING TO RAPID DEVELOPMENT—

HOTELS, RESORTS, GOLF COURSES, SUBDIVISIONS, CONDOS.

HOME PRICES, THE COST OF LIVING, AND TAXES ALL SOARED, AND LOCAL RESIDENTS WERE DISPLACED AND INCREASINGLY EVICTED TO MAKE ROOM FOR HOME BUYERS AND TOURISTS FROM THE MAINLAND.

BY 1970, 80 PERCENT OF LOCAL RESIDENTS COULDN'T AFFORD THE NEW UNITS THAT WERE BEING BUILT.

NATIVE HAWAIIANS, WHO FACED HIGHER UNEMPLOYMENT RATES, HIGHER INCARCERATION RATES, AND LOWER MEDIAN INCOME, WERE DEEPLY AFFECTED.

WHEN DEVELOPERS BEGAN DEMOLISHING THE HOMES LEASED BY LOW-INCOME LOCAL PIG FARMERS IN KALAMA VALLEY IN 1971, TO MAKE WAY FOR A RESORT AREA, SOME RESIDENTS REFUSED TO LEAVE.

THREE DOZEN PROTESTERS JOINED THEM TO FIGHT AGAINST THE FORCED EVICTIONS, DRAWING ATTENTION TO THE ISSUE.

THE TENANTS LOST THEIR BATTLE,
BUT THEIR DEFIANCE KICKED
OFF A MASSIVE WAVE OF

RESISTANCE

BY NATIVE HAWAIIANS WHO HAVE FOUGHT
FOR EVERYTHING FROM RESTITUTION FOR THE
ILLEGAL OVERTHROW OF THE HAWAIIAN KINGDOM, TO ENDING
THE MILITARY OCCUPATION OF SACRED SITES, TO FIGHTING
FOR DRINKING WATER THAT ISN'T POISONED BY TOXIC
RUNOFF FROM SHUTTERED PLANTATIONS AND AGING
MILITARY INSTALLATIONS, TO PROTESTING THE
THIRTY-METER TELESCOPE ON MAUNA KEA,
TO CONSTANT AGITATION FOR
INDEPENDENCE FROM THE UNITED STATES.

ALL THEIR RESISTANCE DRAWS FROM
THE CENTRAL HAWAIIAN BELIEF OF

ALOHA'ĀINA, OR
LOVE OF THE LAND.

AS AMERICAN AS

AS

"THAT'S WHAT THE WHOLE PROCESS IS ABOUT, TO MAKE BEAUTIFUL THINGS OUT OF SOME REALLY TERRIBLE MOMENTS."

—JULIAN SAPORITI, AKA "NO-NO BOY"

THE SIGNS STARTED APPEARING
UP AND DOWN THE WEST COAST
A FEW MONTHS AFTER JAPAN'S
ATTACK ON PEARL HARBOR.

"INSTRUCTIONS TO ALL PERSONS
OF JAPANESE ANCESTRY . . ."
YOU WILL BE **EVACUATED**
FROM THE AREA.

REGISTER HERE. MEET THERE.

NOTICE

BRING ONLY
WHAT YOU
CAN CARRY.

MORE THAN 100,000 PEOPLE
HAD JUST WEEKS TO LIQUIDATE THEIR LIVES.

EVERYONE KNEW THEY HAD TO LEAVE, FAST,
BUT NO ONE KNEW WHERE THEY WERE GOING,
OR HOW LONG THEY'D BE GONE.

SO PEOPLE RUSHED TO FIND A WAY TO FIGURE OUT
HOW TO SELL THE HOMES AND FARMS AND
STORES THEY HAD WORKED SO
HARD TO SECURE.

IN SOME CASES
A SYMPATHETIC
WHITE FRIEND
WOULD OFFER
TO LOOK AFTER
THEM,

BUT IN MOST CASES IT WAS A
MASSIVE FIRE SALE—
CARS, REFRIGERATORS, FURNITURE,
BRAND-NEW CHRISTMAS GIFTS,
BELOVED PETS,

ALL BEING SOLD FOR PENNIES,
GIVEN AWAY, OR STOLEN
BY OPPORTUNISTS.

THE FORCED RELOCATION WAS SPURRED BY
RAMPANT ANTI-JAPANESE SENTIMENT
AND THE RACIST NOTION THAT PEOPLE OF JAPANESE
DESCENT WERE SOMEHOW COMPLICIT WITH JAPAN.

MADE POSSIBLE BY FRANKLIN D. ROOSEVELT'S EXECUTIVE ORDER 9066,
THE WEST COAST WAS DESIGNATED A "MILITARY AREA," WHICH GAVE THE U.S.
GOVERNMENT CONTROL OVER WHO WAS ALLOWED TO EXIST INSIDE OF IT,
AND WHO COULD BE FORCED TO LEAVE.

SURROUNDED BY SEAS OF SUITCASES,
FAMILIES OF ALL AGES, FROM
BABIES TO GRANDMOTHERS,
MOST OF WHOM WERE AMERICAN CITIZENS,
WERE SENT TO "ASSEMBLY CENTERS,"
DIRTY, CROWDED MAKESHIFT HOLDING AREAS
IN CONVERTED RACETRACK STABLES
AND FAIRGROUND FIELDS,
WHILE MORE PERMANENT
INCARCERATION
CAMPS
WERE BEING
BUILT.

(IN EXILE UPON EXILE, SEVERAL OF THE INCARCERATION CAMPS
WERE BUILT ON INDIAN RESERVATIONS, CONSTRUCTED BY
THE U.S. GOVERNMENT DESPITE TRIBAL OPPOSITION.)

BY THE EARLY SUMMER OF 1942, THE TEN "RELOCATION CENTERS" WERE READY, AND SO THOSE AT THE ASSEMBLY CENTERS WERE PUT ONTO HOT, CROWDED TRAINS AND SHIPPED OUT TO REMOTE AREAS ACROSS THE COUNTRY— CENTRAL UTAH, SOUTHEAST ARKANSAS, SOUTHERN IDAHO, NORTHWEST WYOMING.

THE INCARCERATION CAMPS WERE ABYSMAL—

HASTILY CONSTRUCTED, UNINSULATED BARRACKS WITH SHARED OPEN LATRINES, SURROUNDED BY BARBED WIRE AND MACHINE-GUN-WIELDING GUARDS.

THEY WERE DUST-FILLED PRISONS IN THE MIDDLE OF NOWHERE, WITH NO PRIVACY AND NO ESCAPE.

THE NEWLY INCARCERATED WERE SHOCKED AND TERRIFIED. THEY HADN'T DONE ANYTHING WRONG, BUT WERE BEING TREATED LIKE THE ENEMY. NO ONE KNEW HOW LONG THE LIVING NIGHTMARE WOULD LAST, SO THEY SETTLED IN AS BEST THEY COULD.

KIDS WENT TO CAMP SCHOOLS, ADULTS WORKED USING SKILLS THEY HAD, AND LEARNED NEW SKILLS THEY NEEDED—BECOMING LINE COOKS IN THE GIANT MESS HALLS, ACTING AS THE "BLOCKHEADS" WHO PERFORMED BUNK CHECKS.

AS TIME PASSED,
THOSE AT THE CAMPS
FOUND WAYS TO CREATE
COMMUNITY. THEY POSTED
FLYERS INVITING OTHERS
TO JOIN A NEWSPAPER, JOIN
THE BOY SCOUTS, JOIN A CLUB,
JOIN A BAND.

GEORGE IGAWA—
A BANDLEADER FROM LA—
FORMED A SWING BAND AT
THE POMONA ASSEMBLY
CENTER BY SCOUTING OTHER
MUSICIANS WHO ALSO CHOSE
AN INSTRUMENT
AS ONE OF THE FEW
THINGS THEY CARRIED.

CALLING THEMSELVES THE
"POMONANS," WHEN MEMBERS OF
THE GROUP WERE TRANSFERRED
TO HEART MOUNTAIN, THEY
EXPANDED, THIS TIME AS
THE GEORGE IGAWA
ORCHESTRA,
OR G.I. ORCHESTRA.

THE BAND FUSED AMERICAN SWING WITH JAPANESE TUNES AND WAS OPEN TO ANYONE WITH TALENT—SEMI-PROFESSIONALS, PROFESSIONALS, TEENAGERS WITH PROMISE. JOY TAKESHITA, A SIXTEEN-YEAR-OLD, WON A COVETED SPOT AS THE BAND'S VOCALIST. THE ORCHESTRA PRACTICED DAILY, PERFORMING AT HEART MOUNTAIN AND EVEN BEYOND THE CAMP—AT A PROM, A MORMON CHURCH REUNION DANCE, THE AMERICAN LEGION.

MUSIC WAS A FORCE THAT BROUGHT AN

ESCAPE—

AN ESCAPE FROM THE DESOLATION OF BEING INCARCERATED, AN ESCAPE FROM THE CAMP ITSELF, AN ESCAPE FROM BEING SEEN AS A FOREIGN ENEMY WITHIN THEIR OWN COUNTRY.

IN JANUARY OF 1943,
HEART MOUNTAIN HIT ITS
PEAK POPULATION OF NEARLY

ELEVEN THOUSAND,

MAKING IT THE
THIRD-LARGEST
"CITY" IN
WYOMING.

THE ARMY
STARTED
ASKING FOR
JAPANESE
VOLUNTEERS
FOR AN

ALL-JAPANESE SEGREGATED ARMY UNIT.

INCARCEREES WERE GIVEN

A "LOYALTY QUESTIONNAIRE,"

FILLED WITH PROBING QUESTIONS THAT
SOUGHT TO GET AT WHETHER INCARCEREES
SAW THEMSELVES AS

"JAPANESE" OR "AMERICAN."

THE LOYALTY QUESTIONS CAUGHT MANY IN A BIND,
ESPECIALLY QUESTION 27, WHICH ASKED IF INCARCEREES WOULD
SERVE ON COMBAT DUTY, AND QUESTION 28, WHICH ASKED IF THEY
WOULD RENOUNCE ANY ALLEGIANCE TO JAPAN AND SWEAR
ALLEGIANCE TO THE UNITED STATES.

WOULD ANSWERING YES TO 27 BE AKIN TO SIGNING UP FOR ACTIVE DUTY? WOULD JAPANESE IMMIGRANTS BE LEFT STATELESS IF THEY RENOUNCED JAPAN, BUT STILL COULDN'T BECOME AMERICAN CITIZENS DUE TO RACIST IMMIGRATION LAWS? WOULD THEY BE PUNISHED WITH SOLITARY CONFINEMENT FOR ANSWERING NO?

THE VAST MAJORITY ANSWERED YES. SOME VOLUNTARILY ENLISTED IN THE ARMY, AND OTHERS WERE LATER DRAFTED.

NOT EVERYONE ANSWERED YES, THOUGH.

SOME SAID NO, SOME QUALIFIED THEIR RESPONSE, SOME REFUSED TO ANSWER. AT HEART MOUNTAIN A GROUP CALLED THE FAIR PLAY COMMITTEE RESISTED BY STATING THAT THEY WOULDN'T ANSWER YES UNTIL THEIR

FULL RIGHTS AS AMERICAN CITIZENS WERE RESTORED.

THOSE WHO RESISTED BECAME KNOWN AS "NO-NO BOYS"
AND POST-WAR WERE SHUNNED BOTH BY THE JAPANESE AMERICAN
COMMUNITY AND THE WIDER AMERICAN PUBLIC AS TRAITORS.

BUT MORE RECENTLY, THEIR LEGACY, ALONG WITH THE LEGACY
OF JAPANESE INTERNMENT, IS BEING RE-EXPLORED.

MUSICIAN AND SCHOLAR JULIAN SAPORITI
PERFORMS AS "NO-NO BOY," CREATING MUSIC
AND MULTIMEDIA STORYTELLING PROJECTS
THAT BRING HISTORY TO LIFE THROUGH SONG.

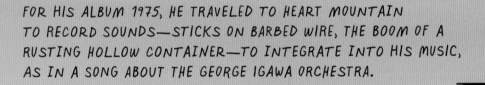

FOR HIS ALBUM 1975, HE TRAVELED TO HEART MOUNTAIN
TO RECORD SOUNDS—STICKS ON BARBED WIRE, THE BOOM OF A
RUSTING HOLLOW CONTAINER—TO INTEGRATE INTO HIS MUSIC,
AS IN A SONG ABOUT THE GEORGE IGAWA ORCHESTRA.

SAPORITI USES HIS MUSIC TO DRAW CONNECTIONS IN ALL DIRECTIONS—FROM JAPANESE INTERNMENT, TO HIS OWN AMERICAN IDENTITY, TO THE IMMIGRANTS AND REFUGEES STILL STRUGGLING IN AMERICAN INCARCERATION CAMPS TODAY.

"HISTORY IS A MESS THAT DOESN'T MAKE SENSE, AND THAT'S KIND OF WHERE I LEAVE IT," SAPORITI SAYS.

"THAT'S WHY SONGS ARE SUCH A WONDERFUL WAY TO DEAL WITH IT, BECAUSE YOU CAN JUST SIT WITH THE MESS, AND YOU CAN SING THROUGH THE MESS, AND MAYBE BY DOING THAT YOU REFLECT AND CAN SHINE SOME KIND OF LIGHT ON WHAT'S HAPPENING TODAY. WHEN IT DOES REPEAT ITSELF. WHEN THOSE

ECHOES BECOME RESONANT."

THE OLD
BALLGAME

"WORDS ARE EVENTS, THEY DO THINGS, CHANGE THINGS."

—URSULA K. LE GUIN

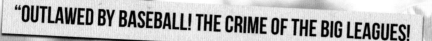

Daily Worker

Entered as second-class matter at the Post Office at New York, N. Y., under the act of March 3, 1879.

"OUTLAWED BY BASEBALL! THE CRIME OF THE BIG LEAGUES!

THE NEWSPAPERS HAVE CAREFULLY HUSHED IT UP!

ONE OF THE MOST SORDID STORIES IN AMERICAN SPORTS!

IN THE SUMMER OF 1936,
THE DAILY WORKER
(THE OFFICIAL NEWSPAPER OF
THE COMMUNIST PARTY IN THE U.S.)
PROMISED READERS AN EXPOSÉ
THAT WOULD BE "MENTIONING NAMES, GIVING
FACTS, SPARING NONE OF THE MOST SACRED
FIGURES IN BASEBALL OFFICIALDOM."

THE FOCUS?
FORCED SEGREGATION
IN BASEBALL.

THE PAPER HAMMERED HARD ON THE ISSUE,
EDUCATING FANS ABOUT BASEBALL'S
RIGIDLY ENFORCED COLOR LINE,
AND URGING THEM TO SPEAK OUT AGAINST IT.

THE CALL WAS A NEW ONE. UP UNTIL THAT POINT
THE DAILY WORKER'S SPORTS COVERAGE HAD BEEN
DRY AND DISMISSIVE.
SPORTS LIKE BASEBALL, THEY
WROTE, WERE JUST THERE TO
DISTRACT WORKERS FROM
THEIR MISERABLE CONDITIONS.

BUT LESTER RODNEY, A YOUNG JEWISH NIGHT STUDENT AT
NEW YORK UNIVERSITY, ADORED BASEBALL AND THOUGHT
THE PAPER COULD DO BETTER.
WHEN HE TOLD THEM SO, HE WAS HIRED AND GIVEN FREE REIN
TO BOTH CELEBRATE AND CRITICIZE THE SPORT.

THE RESULT WAS COVERAGE THAT WAS
RADICALLY DIFFERENT
FROM OTHER SPORTS REPORTING AT THE TIME—
IT OPENLY DISCUSSED RACE AND POWER AND FOCUSED
ON THE INFLUENCE FANS HAD TO MAKE CHANGE.

BASEBALL

WAS AMERICA'S

NATIONAL PASTIME,

AND THE MAJOR PAPERS COVERED THE MAJOR
LEAGUES AS IF THEY WERE JUST NATURALLY

AN ALL-WHITE AFFAIR.

THERE WERE SEGREGATED "NEGRO LEAGUES"
WHERE TALENTED BLACK ATHLETES
PLAYED BASEBALL. THEY WERE
UPLIFTED BY THE BLACK PRESS
AND ADORED BY
BLACK FANS,

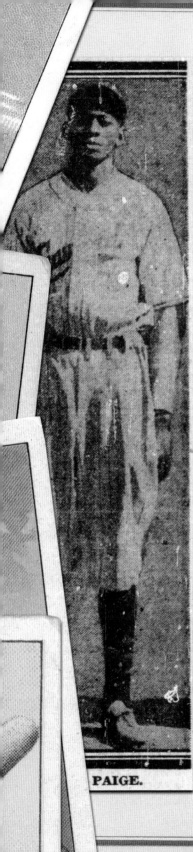

PAIGE.

BUT THE WHITE, MAINSTREAM PRESS
LARGELY IGNORED THEM.

RODNEY THOUGHT THE
SILENCE WAS INEXCUSABLE
AND HE DEDICATED HIS SPORTS PAGE
**TO EXPOSING HOW SEGREGATION
WAS CRAFTED AND MAINTAINED.**

HE DID THOROUGH, INVESTIGATIVE REPORTING TO
SCOUT AND HIGHLIGHT GREAT BLACK BALLPLAYERS,
COLLABORATED WITH BLACK SPORTSWRITERS,
GOT COMMISSIONERS TO CONFIRM THERE WAS
NO WRITTEN LAW
THAT EXPLICITLY BARRED BLACK TALENT
(ONLY A 19TH-CENTURY "GENTLEMEN'S AGREEMENT"
THAT CONTINUED TO BE UPHELD), AND GOT
WHITE BALLPLAYERS ON THE RECORD SAYING
THEY'D BE FINE WITH INTEGRATION.

HE'D PRINT WHAT OTHER WHITE REPORTERS
WOULDN'T, OR COULDN'T,
DEPENDING ON THEIR PAPERS AND EDITORS.

WHEN, FOR EXAMPLE, JOE DIMAGGIO QUIPPED IN 1937
TO A GAGGLE OF REPORTERS THAT HE THOUGHT
SATCHEL PAIGE
WAS THE BEST PITCHER HE'D EVER FACED,
NOT A SINGLE OTHER OUTLET RAN WITH THE
REMARK EXCEPT FOR RODNEY
(AS A MASSIVE HEADLINE).

INSPIRED BY THE REPORTING, YOUNG COMMUNIST LEAGUE MEMBERS HANDED OUT LEAFLETS AT YANKEE STADIUM, EBBETS FIELD, AND THE POLO GROUNDS, EXPLAINING THE ISSUE, AND RAISING THE CONSCIOUSNESS OF WHITE FANS.

THEY COLLECTED 1.5 MILLION SIGNATURES IN SUPPORT OF INTEGRATION,

AND IN 1938, UNIONS CARRIED BANNERS THAT READ "END JIM CROW IN BASEBALL" DURING THE COMMUNIST PARTY'S ANNUAL MAY DAY PARADE.

MANY OF THOSE RODNEY WORKED WITH WERE ALSO
JEWISH, AND THEIR WORK WAS PART OF A TRADITION
OF JEWS, ESPECIALLY JEWS IN THE COMMUNIST PARTY,
WORKING IN SOLIDARITY WITH THE BLACK COMMUNITY
TO COMBAT ANTI-BLACK RACISM.

RODNEY KEPT
PUSHING,
REPORTING
RELENTLESSLY
ON THE
COLOR LINE
IN BASEBALL
FOR THE
NEXT
DECADE.

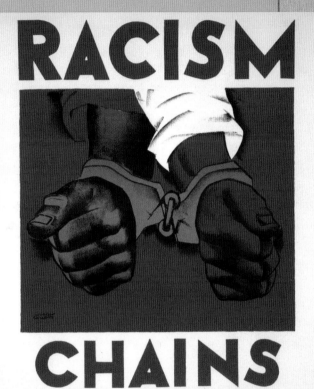

RACISM CHAINS BOTH

Communist Party USA
National Black Liberation Commission
23 West 26" Street, New York, N.Y., 10010

BY THE MID-1940S, OTHER JEWISH REPORTERS AT MAJOR PAPERS—
LIKE WALTER WINCHELL AND SHIRLEY POVICH OF THE WASHINGTON
POST AND ROGER KAHN OF THE NEW YORK HERALD TRIBUNE—
ALSO BEGAN TO VIGOROUSLY PUSH FOR INTEGRATION.

FINALLY, THE COLOR
LINE WAS OFFICIALLY
BROKEN IN 1947 WHEN
**JACKIE
ROBINSON**
STARTED AT FIRST
BASE FOR THE
**BROOKLYN
DODGERS.**

FOR THE FIRST
FEW YEARS,
WHITE BALLPLAYERS
SUBJECTED ROBINSON TO
CONSTANT ABUSE—HE WAS
STRUCK INTENTIONALLY
BY BALLS, INSULTED,
AND CONTINUOUSLY
PROVOKED.

JEWISH PLAYERS, LIKE HANK GREENBERG,
RALLIED AROUND ROBINSON,
AND ROBINSON BECAME A
JEWISH ICON
AS MUCH AS THE JEWISH
BASEBALL PLAYERS
WERE.

TOWARD THE END OF HIS LIFE WHEN HE
WAS IN HIS NINETIES, RODNEY SAID HE STILL
GOT CHOKED UP THINKING
ABOUT ALL THE TALENT THAT
HAD BEEN STIFLED BY APARTHEID—
JOSH GIBSON, SATCHEL PAIGE, CHARLIE GRANT,
JOHN HENRY LLOYD, COUNTLESS OTHERS WHO NEVER
GOT TO FULFILL THEIR POTENTIAL.

"IT'S AN AMERICAN TRAGEDY,"
HE SAID.

DOWN ON THE FARM

"EVERY MOMENT IS AN ORGANIZING OPPORTUNITY,
EVERY PERSON A POTENTIAL ACTIVIST,
EVERY MINUTE A CHANCE TO CHANGE THE WORLD."

—DOLORES HUERTA

IN THE SUMMER OF 1965, ELDER FILIPINO FARMWORKERS
HARVESTING GRAPES IN CALIFORNIA'S COACHELLA VALLEY
HAD HAD ENOUGH. AGAIN.

KNOWN AS MANONGS—WHICH AFFECTIONATELY MEANS OLDER
BROTHER—THE FIFTY-, SIXTY-, AND SEVENTY-YEAR-OLD MEN
HAD BEEN WORKING THE FIELDS AND AGITATING FOR
BETTER WORKING CONDITIONS FOR DECADES.

FRUSTRATED THAT THEY WERE MAKING
THIRTY CENTS LESS THAN BRACEROS—
TEMPORARY MEXICAN WORKERS BROUGHT ACROSS THE
BORDER BY THE U.S. GOVERNMENT TO PROVIDE GROWERS
WITH EXPLOITABLE LABOR—

THEY ORGANIZED A WORK STOPPAGE
VIA THEIR UNION,

THE AGRICULTURAL WORKERS ORGANIZING COMMITTEE
(AWOC), AND DEMANDED THEIR WAGES BE RAISED
TO $1.40 AN HOUR.

THEY QUICKLY SUCCEEDED, BUT
WORKING CONDITIONS REMAINED ABYSMAL.

THEY WERE DENIED BASICS
LIKE AMPLE DRINKING WATER AND ACCESSIBLE BATHROOMS.
THEY HAD NO WORKERS' COMP, NO SOCIAL SECURITY,
NO HOURLY CAPS, NO OVERTIME, NO RULES ALLOWING
THEM TO SLOW DOWN WHEN THE WEATHER
SOARED OVER 100 DEGREES.

A RAISE WAS GOOD,
BUT IT WAS ALSO TEMPORARY
WITHOUT A UNIVERSAL CONTRACT ALL GROWERS RESPECTED.

LATER THAT SUMMER WHEN THE MANONGS FOLLOWED THE GROWING SEASON AND MOVED NORTH TO DELANO, CALIFORNIA, NORTHERN GROWERS REFUSED TO PAY THE HIGHER WAGE.

SO AWOC FARMWORKERS, LED BY LARRY ITLIONG, **DECIDED TO STRIKE.**

ON SEPTEMBER 8, THEY WENT TO THE FIELDS LIKE ANY OTHER DAY AND WORKED, HARVESTING GRAPES FROM THE VINE.

THEN AT NOON, 1,500 OF THEM STOPPED AND WALKED OFF THE FIELDS IN UNISON, LEAVING THE GRAPES ON THE GROUND.

THE GROWERS WERE IRATE, AND RETALIATED.

THEY TURNED OFF THE LIGHTS, WATER, AND GAS
IN THE LABOR CAMPS WHERE THE WORKERS LIVED.
THE STRIKING FARMWORKERS WERE HARASSED BY THE POLICE; SOME WERE BEATEN.

FIVE DAYS INTO THE STRIKE, GROWERS STARTED TO BRING IN **MEXICAN FARMWORKERS** AS STRIKEBREAKERS.

IT WAS A LONG-USED TACTIC—CALIFORNIA GROWERS HAD A HISTORY OF SEGREGATING ETHNIC GROUPS AND THEN PITTING THEM AGAINST ONE ANOTHER TO ENSURE A STEADY STREAM OF **CHEAP, EXPENDABLE LABOR.**

ITLIONG DECIDED THE ONLY WAY TO WIN BETTER WORKING CONDITIONS **FOR EVERYONE** WAS TO BAND TOGETHER, SO HE WENT TO CESAR CHAVEZ, WHO HAD BEEN ORGANIZING THE MEXICAN WORKERS ALONGSIDE DOLORES HUERTA AND GILBERT PADILLA AS PART OF THE NATIONAL FARM WORKERS ASSOCIATION (NFWA).

CHAVEZ WAS HESITANT. HE AGREED WITH ITLIONG'S AIMS,
BUT DIDN'T THINK THE NFWA WAS READY FOR A STRIKE.

THE ORGANIZATION ONLY HAD $100 IN THE BANK,
AND A STRIKE WAS RISKY: WORKERS STOOD TO BE BLACKLISTED
BY GROWERS, AND MOST HAD FAMILIES TO FEED AND SUPPORT.
BUT ITLIONG PRESSED.

SO A WEEK AFTER AWOC'S STRIKE BEGAN,
CHAVEZ ASKED HIS OWN MEMBERS TO VOTE.

THE VOTE WAS UNANIMOUS;
THEY JOINED THE STRIKE.

ALTHOUGH POWERFUL,
IT WAS A TENUOUS
UNION.
THE AWOC AND NFWA WERE
DIFFERENT ORGANIZATIONS,
WITH DIFFERENT
PHILOSOPHIES AND PERSONALITIES.

AWOC WAS KNOWN AS BRINGING TOGETHER
A DIVERSE COALITION OF FILIPINO,
BLACK, MEXICAN, AND WHITE
FARMWORKERS (THE "OKIES" WHO
FLED TO CALIFORNIA WHEN THE
DUST BOWL DROVE THEM FROM
THE MIDWEST).

ITLIONG HIMSELF BECAME AN IMMIGRANT FARMWORKER AT **FIFTEEN,** AND WAS KNOWN AS A CHARISMATIC, LOUD, AND BRASH LEADER.

THE NFWA WAS **PREDOMINATELY CHICANO** AND MANY MEMBERS ONLY **SPOKE SPANISH.**

CHAVEZ AND HUERTA WERE ALSO DEEPLY CONNECTED WITH THE FARMWORKER COMMUNITY—BOTH OF THEM HAD PARENTS WHO HAD BEEN FARMWORKERS— BUT THEY WERE MORE EDUCATED, MORE FAMILIAR WITH THE INNER WORKINGS OF POLITICS, AND **MORE MEDIA SAVVY.**

DESPITE THEIR DIFFERENCES, EVERYONE GATHERED AT THE FILIPINO HALL IN DELANO AND BEGAN DELIBERATING ON THE BEST WAY TO SUSTAIN THE STRIKE **IN ORDER TO ESTABLISH BETTER WORKING CONDITIONS FOR ALL.**

THE GROUPS OFFICIALLY MERGED TO CREATE THE
UNITED FARM WORKERS OF AMERICA (UFW),
AND PULLED IN SUPPORT FROM OTHER UNIONS.

SOME, LIKE THE POWERFUL UNITED AUTO WORKERS, GAVE MONEY TO HELP FEED
AND CARE FOR THE STRIKERS, AND OTHERS, LIKE THE INTERNATIONAL LONGSHORE
AND WAREHOUSE UNION, GAVE THEIR POWER, REFUSING TO LOAD GRAPES
THAT HAD BEEN PICKED BY STRIKEBREAKERS ONTO SHIPS FOR DISTRIBUTION,
LEAVING THEM TO ROT ON THE DOCKS.

THE UFW REACHED OUT LOCALLY, AND STUDENTS FROM SURROUNDING SCHOOLS
HELD BAKE SALES AND DANCES AND CANNED FOOD DRIVES IN SUPPORT.

THEY REACHED OUT TO CELEBRITIES, AND SINGERS LIKE PETE SEEGER
GAVE CONCERTS AND DONATED THE PROCEEDS.

THEY ORGANIZED MASS ACTIONS, LIKE A 300-MILE MARCH
FROM DELANO TO SACRAMENTO, WHERE STRIKERS SANG, DANCED,
AND CALLED IN FARMWORKERS FROM THE FIELDS TO JOIN THEM.
SEVENTY FARMWORKERS AND VOLUNTEERS
BEGAN THE MARCH.

BY THE END, THEY WERE 10,000 SUPPORTERS STRONG.

THE MESSAGE GOT MORE SUCCINCT:
"FARMWORKERS ARE ON STRIKE, DON'T BUY GRAPES;
DON'T SHOP AT STORES THAT BUY GRAPES."

CONSUMERS ACROSS THE COUNTRY TOOK ACTION.

BLACK AND PUERTO RICAN COMMUNITIES DID AWAY WITH GRAPES FIRST.
BY THE HEIGHT OF THE BOYCOTT 17 MILLION PEOPLE HAD STOPPED EATING GRAPES.

THE GROWERS WERE ENRAGED.

THEY HIRED MEN TO TERRORIZE FARMWORKERS WHO WERE VOTING
TO UNIONIZE. THEY WORKED WITH SHERIFFS, WHO BEAT UP AND ARRESTED
PROTESTORS AND STRIKERS. THEY WON THE FAVOR OF POLITICIANS LIKE
CALIFORNIA GOVERNOR RONALD REAGAN, WHO WOULD EAT GRAPES ON
CAMERA TO SIGNAL HIS DISDAIN FOR THE BOYCOTT.

BUT THE STRIKE PERSEVERED.

FINALLY, IN 1970, FIVE YEARS AFTER THE STRIKE BEGAN, THE UFW REACHED A HISTORIC **COLLECTIVE BARGAINING** AGREEMENT WITH GROWERS THAT BROUGHT FARMWORKERS HEALTH AND RETIREMENT BENEFITS, A LIVABLE MINIMUM WAGE SET TO RISE YEAR OVER YEAR, SECURE JOB ASSIGNMENTS, AND A WAY TO SUBMIT GRIEVANCES FOR **50,000 MEMBERS.**

THE FARMWORKERS DIDN'T ONLY ASK FOR THINGS THAT HELPED THEMSELVES.

FOR YEARS, WORKERS HAD KNOWN THAT THE PESTICIDES BEING USED ON GRAPES, LIKE DDT, WERE MAKING THEIR FAMILIES SICK.

THEY WANTED THE PUBLIC TO KNOW, AND THEY WANTED TO PROTECT THEM TOO.

SO THEIR CONTRACTS WITH GROWERS ALSO BANNED THE USE OF FIVE HARMFUL PESTICIDES, YEARS BEFORE THE FEDERAL GOVERNMENT ACTED TO DO SO.

TODAY, THE DELANO GRAPE STRIKE IS CONSIDERED ONE OF **THE MOST SUCCESSFUL UNION BOYCOTTS EVER,** A FORERUNNER OF THE ENVIRONMENTAL JUSTICE MOVEMENT, THE TRIGGER OF THE CHICANO MOVEMENT, AND THE FORCE THAT AWAKENED LATINE POLITICAL POWER.

IT'S ALSO FINALLY BEING CELEBRATED MORE WIDELY AS A CRITICAL MOVEMENT IN FILIPINO AMERICAN HISTORY, WITH ACTIVISTS PUSHING TO **RECENTER ITLIONG'S LEADERSHIP.**

STILL, THE STRUGGLE OF MIGRANT FARMWORKERS CONTINUES.

THE ESTIMATED TWO MILLION WORKERS REMAIN SOME OF THE POOREST IN THE COUNTRY. **MORE THAN HALF ARE UNDOCUMENTED** AND HAVE NO LEGAL STATUS, OPENING THEM UP TO ABUSE. PROGRAMS LIKE THE H-2A SEASONAL GUEST WORKERS VISA MIRROR THE EXPLOITATIVE BRACERO PROGRAM. WORKERS ARE STILL PLAGUED BY PESTICIDES, SUBSTANDARD HOUSING, A LACK OF JOB SECURITY.

SO THE UFW FIGHTS ON.

MADE IN AMERICA

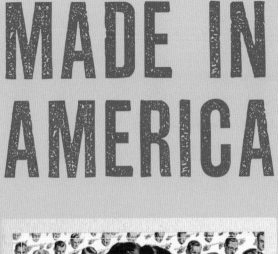

"THE ELEMENTS OF NATURE ARE A LIMITLESS FRONTIER, A CONTINUING CHALLENGE TO SCIENCE."

—1954 CHEMICAL COMPANY ADVERTISEMENT

LOOKING AT THE CITY OF
NIAGARA FALLS FROM ABOVE,
THERE ARE BLANK SPOTS.

TREELESS, GRASSY, OBLONG SHAPES.

THEY BUTT UP AGAINST BACK LOT STRIP
MALLS AND FREEWAYS AND SMALL
SIDE STREETS.

THEY'RE EASY
TO IGNORE.

BUT UP CLOSE, THEY'RE
BAD IMPERSONATIONS
OF NATURE.

SOME ARE MARKED.

SOME ARE
NOT.

ALL ARE
FILLED WITH
**TOXIC
WASTE.**

THE CITY OF NIAGARA FALLS IS NAMED FOR
THE FAMOUS WATERFALL IT'S BUILT AROUND,
A WONDER OF THE WORLD.

WITH SIX MILLION
CUBIC FEET OF WATER
RUSHING OVER THE EDGE
EVERY MINUTE, THE FALLS
HAVE LONG BEEN

ASSOCIATED WITH

POWER.

PEOPLE HAVE LIVED AROUND ITS BANKS SINCE
ITS CREATION NEARLY 12,000 YEARS AGO, BUT
ONLY IN THE LAST 350 OR SO SINCE THE FIRST
WHITE SETTLERS SHOWED UP HAVE PEOPLE TRIED

TO HARNESS THE FALLS'
POWER FOR PROFIT.

IN THE 1750S, DANIEL JONCAIRE CREATED A SHORT MILLRACE—A CHANNEL THAT DIVERTED SOME OF THE RUSHING WATER ABOVE THE FALLS—TO POWER HIS SAWMILL.

A SMATTERING OF OTHER BUSINESSES JOINED JONCAIRE—PAPER MILLS, PULP MILLS, FLOUR MILLS.

BUT IT WASN'T UNTIL 1877, WHEN JOSEPH SCHOELLKOPF PURCHASED A 4,500-FOOT HYDRAULIC CANAL AND MADE IMPROVEMENTS VIA A SERIES OF TUNNELS THAT NIAGARA FALLS INDUSTRY TRULY BOOMED.

IN 1881, THE FIRST ELECTRIC GENERATOR POWERED BY THE CANAL'S WATER WAS BUILT, AND FIVE YEARS LATER THE NIAGARA FALLS POWER COMPANY WAS THE GREATEST HYDROELECTRIC ENTERPRISE IN THE WORLD.

CHEAP AND CONTINUOUS ELECTRIC POWER ATTRACTED
BUDDING ELECTRO-PROCESS INDUSTRIES LIKE

CHEMICAL COMPANIES,

WHICH NEEDED TONS OF ELECTRICITY TO MANUFACTURE THEIR PRODUCTS—
SILICON CARBIDE, ALUMINUM, CHLORINE, POLYESTER RESINS, DDT, PVC.

FROM THE EARLY 1900S INTO THE 1950S, THE CHEMICALS
NIAGARA FALLS' COMPANIES INVENTED AND PRODUCED WERE

USED TO MANUFACTURE MODERN LIFE—

GLASS, SOAP, FERTILIZER, EXPLOSIVES, PHARMACEUTICALS.

FOR CONSUMERS, THE COMPANIES WERE ASSOCIATED
WITH PROGRESS AND BETTER LIVING, AND THE
PRODUCTS THEY POWERED SEEMED LIKE MAGIC—

JET PLANES, WARM HOMES, RADIOS, VACUUM CLEANERS, MEDICINE.

THE COMPANIES, THEIR
WORKERS, AND LOCAL RESIDENTS,
HOWEVER, KNEW THAT MAGIC
EXTRACTED A PRICE.

IT WAS AN OPEN
SECRET THE CITY
WAS BEING USED
AS A DUMP.

THE CHEMICAL COMPANIES
PRODUCED SO MUCH WASTE,
THEY CHUCKED IT HOWEVER
THEY COULD, INCLUDING
GIVING WORKERS $50 EACH
IN THE 1940S TO TAKE
A DRUM HOME
AND MAKE IT
DISAPPEAR.

BY THE 1960S, NIAGARA FALLS RESIDENTS STARTED COMPLAINING ABOUT STRANGE SMELLS AND EXPOSED WASTE AROUND THE CITY.

BY THE 1970S, FAMILIES IN THE NIAGARA FALLS NEIGHBORHOOD OF LOVE CANAL REPORTED KIDS GETTING CHEMICAL BURNS WHILE PLAYING BASEBALL, NOXIOUS FUMES RISING UP THROUGH THEIR BASEMENTS, ROCKS SUDDENLY EXPLODING LIKE FIRECRACKERS, CATS MYSTERIOUSLY DYING, PEOPLE GETTING SICK.

UNBEKNOWNST TO THE NEIGHBORHOOD'S RESIDENTS, THEIR HOMES AND THE LOCAL PUBLIC SCHOOL HAD BEEN BUILT DIRECTLY ON TOP OF HOOKER CHEMICALS' DUMPING GROUND FILLED WITH 21,000 TONS OF IMPROPERLY STORED, HIGHLY TOXIC CHEMICAL WASTE.

LOIS GIBBS, A LOCAL MOM, RALLIED NEIGHBORS TO JOIN FORCES AND DEMAND JUSTICE AFTER HER FIVE-YEAR-OLD SON GOT SICK. MICHAEL BROWN AT THE NIAGARA GAZETTE COVERED THE STORY EXTENSIVELY AND BY 1978 LOVE CANAL WAS NATIONAL NEWS.

A STATE OF EMERGENCY WAS DECLARED, AND THE NEW YORK STATE HEALTH COMMISSIONER RECOMMENDED PREGNANT WOMEN AND SMALL CHILDREN EVACUATE THE AREA, BUT MOST COULDN'T AFFORD TO MOVE SINCE THEIR HOMES WERE NOW ESSENTIALLY WORTHLESS.

NEIGHBORHOOD ACTIVISTS KEPT RALLYING. IN 1980 THE SUPERFUND PROGRAM—A FEDERAL INITIATIVE TO CLEAN UP CONTAMINATED SITES—WAS ESTABLISHED, AND ENVIRONMENTAL REGULATIONS WERE TIGHTENED. THE FEDERAL GOVERNMENT PROVIDED AID TO HELP CLEAN UP THE CITY, AND RESIDENTS REACHED A SETTLEMENT WITH HOOKER.

AFTER LOVE CANAL, HUNDREDS OF SUPERFUND SITES
WERE IDENTIFIED ACROSS THE COUNTRY.

ROCKY FLATS IN COLORADO, WHERE THE U.S. GOVERNMENT HAD
MANUFACTURED PLUTONIUM FOR NUCLEAR WEAPONS;

SILVER BOW CREEK IN MONTANA, WHERE 100 YEARS OF
MINING WASTE HAD SOAKED INTO STREAMS AND SOIL;

METAMORA, MICHIGAN, WHERE INDUSTRIAL WASTE AND
MUNICIPAL WASTE HAD ACCUMULATED OVER DECADES
IN A PRIVATE, UNREGULATED OPEN DUMP.

THE ENVIRONMENTAL PROTECTION AGENCY
BEGAN THE SLOW AND STEADY
PROCESS OF REMEDIATION.
ANALYZING, CONTAINING, AND CLEANING OUT THE WASTE.

BUT TOXIC WASTE DOESN'T
JUST DISAPPEAR.
IT HAS TO BE REMOVED
TO SOMEWHERE.

BY THE LATE 1980S, THE CITY OF
NIAGARA FALLS WAS NOT ONLY REMEDIATING
ITS OWN TOXIC WASTE, BUT THE WASTE OF THE
ENTIRE NORTHEASTERN UNITED STATES.

HOME TO A BRANCH OF CHEMICAL WASTE
MANAGEMENT—THE LARGEST HAZARDOUS
WASTE DISPOSAL COMPANY IN NORTH AMERICA—
NIAGARA FALLS HAD ONE OF THE FEW LANDFILLS
LICENSED TO ACCEPT THE TOXIC SLUDGE
NO ONE ELSE WOULD KEEP.

EVEN WHEN LOVE CANAL ITSELF WAS
CLEANED UP, THE TOXINS WERE
TRUCKED JUST FIFTEEN MINUTES SOUTH.

AGAIN, THERE WERE HOUSES
RIGHT NEXT TO IT.

AGAIN, RESIDENTS GOT SICK.

BUT IT'S DIFFICULT TO CONCLUSIVELY PROVE THAT PEOPLE'S ILLNESSES ARE **DIRECTLY TIED** TO A COMPANY'S WASTE.

CANCERS TAKE A LONG TIME TO DEVELOP; PEOPLE OFTEN MOVE AND DO OTHER CANCER-CAUSING THINGS LIKE SMOKE CIGARETTES AND GO TO TANNING SALONS.

IN 2017, NANCY B. BECK, A TRUMP ADMINISTRATION APPOINTEE TO THE ENVIRONMENTAL PROTECTION AGENCY'S TOXIC CHEMICAL UNIT, BEMOANED THAT **OBSESSING OVER "PHANTOM RISKS"** CAN CREATE **"TREMENDOUS COSTS"** FOR CHEMICAL COMPANIES.

SO THE AGENCY DECIDED TO TAKE A "NEW DIRECTION ON LEGACY CHEMICALS"— **LESS** REGULATION, LESS DIGGING INTO LONG-TERM HEALTH HAZARDS.

TODAY,

NIAGARA FALLS'
POPULATION HAS

PLUMMETED
TO HALF

WHAT IT WAS AT
ITS HEIGHT IN 1960.

**ALMOST ONE IN
TWO RESIDENTS LIVE
IN POVERTY.**

IT HAS ONE OF THE
STATE'S HIGHEST MORTALITY
RATES AND NOTABLY ELEVATED
CANCER RATES, WITH SPECIFIC
CANCERS (SUCH AS BLADDER)
CLUSTERED AROUND SPECIFIC
PLANTS (LIKE GOODYEAR).

**THE CITY IS TRYING TO MOVE
AWAY FROM ITS TOXIC LEGACY
AND DOUBLE DOWN ON TOURISM.**

IN 2011, NEW YORK LAUNCHED A $150 MILLION
REVITALIZATION EFFORT TO STEADILY IMPROVE
VIEWING AREAS AND WALKWAYS, AND IN 2021,
PROPOSED A NEW $46 MILLION VISITOR CENTER.

ALL THE WHILE, RADIOACTIVE
MATERIAL KEEPS BEING FOUND—

UNDER BOWLING ALLEYS AND BUILDING SUPPLY STORES,
IN PEOPLE'S DRIVEWAYS AND FLOWER BEDS.

STREETS PAVED WITH GOLD

"THAT'S WHY THEY CALL IT THE AMERICAN DREAM, BECAUSE YOU HAVE TO BE ASLEEP TO BELIEVE IT."

—GEORGE CARLIN

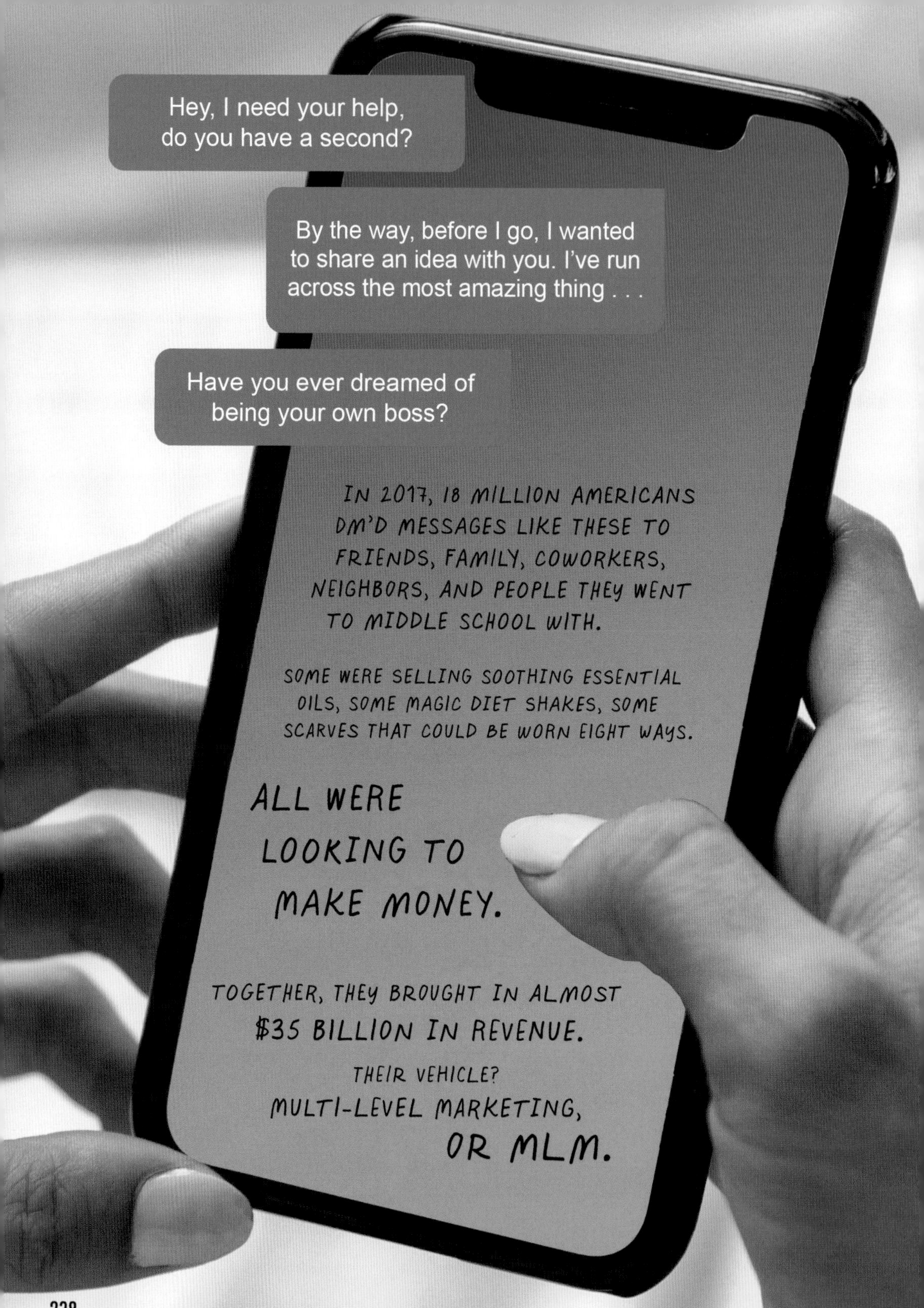
Hey, I need your help, do you have a second?
By the way, before I go, I wanted to share an idea with you. I've run across the most amazing thing . . .
Have you ever dreamed of being your own boss?
IN 2017, 18 MILLION AMERICANS DM'D MESSAGES LIKE THESE TO FRIENDS, FAMILY, COWORKERS, NEIGHBORS, AND PEOPLE THEY WENT TO MIDDLE SCHOOL WITH.
SOME WERE SELLING SOOTHING ESSENTIAL OILS, SOME MAGIC DIET SHAKES, SOME SCARVES THAT COULD BE WORN EIGHT WAYS.
ALL WERE LOOKING TO MAKE MONEY.
TOGETHER, THEY BROUGHT IN ALMOST $35 BILLION IN REVENUE.
THEIR VEHICLE?
MULTI-LEVEL MARKETING, OR MLM.

THE ORIGIN OF THE MLM MODEL IS DISPUTED.

IT MIGHT HAVE STARTED IN THE 1860S WITH HEINZ KETCHUP, OR J.R. WATKINS SKIN CREAMS.

OR IT MAY HAVE BEEN WHEN P. F. E. ALBEE BECAME THE ORIGINAL AVON LADY IN THE 1880S BY RECRUITING A GAGGLE OF SALESWOMEN TO SELL PERFUME, EFFECTIVELY KICKING OFF

WOMAN-TO-WOMAN SELLING.

REGARDLESS, BY THE MID-20TH CENTURY, THE NOTION OF MAKING MONEY NOT JUST BY SELLING STUFF BUT BY

CONVINCING OTHERS TO BECOME SELLERS TO SELL EVEN

MORE STUFF

HAD BECOME A DISTINCTLY AMERICAN BUSINESS MODEL.

BY THE 1970S,
THE REIGNING MLM CHAMP
WAS A COMPANY THAT EMBODIED
THE FERVOR OF FREE ENTERPRISE,
POSITIVE THINKING,
AND PATRIOTISM SO DEEPLY
IT CALLED ITSELF "THE
AMERICAN WAY,"
OR AMWAY FOR SHORT.

THE COMPANY WAS PRAISED BY
PRESIDENTS—GERALD FORD
CALLED IT "A VIBRANT FORCE
OF GOOD"—AND ITS FOUNDERS
WERE SEEN AS GODLY MEN—
REVEREND BILLY GRAHAM HAILED
COFOUNDER RICH DEVOS AS

**"ONE OF THE MOST
DEDICATED CHRISTIAN
LAYMEN I HAVE
EVER KNOWN."**

AMWAY SOLD LIQUID CLEANER.

BUT IT WAS NEVER ABOUT THE CLEANER (OR THE OTHER 150 RANDOM "EVERYDAY PRODUCTS" THE COMPANY HAWKED).

IT WAS ABOUT THE AMERICAN DREAM.

AMWAY SOLD *OPPORTUNITY* ITSELF.

EVERY AMERICAN—FROM SINGLE MOMS TO MARRIED COUPLES, TRUCK DRIVERS TO DOCTORS—COULD GET SUPER RICH. THEY JUST (AMWAY SAID) HAD TO WORK HARD, AND REALLY, REALLY *WANT TO SUCCEED.*

AMWAY SALESPEOPLE WERE USUALLY BROUGHT INTO THE FOLD, OR "SPONSORED," BY **SOMEONE THEY KNEW**— *THEIR FRIEND, THEIR FATHER'S COWORKER, THEIR HAIRDRESSER.*

THE COMPANY ENCOURAGED PEOPLE TO TRANSFORM **THEIR PERSONAL RELATIONSHIPS INTO TRANSACTIONAL ONES**—

TO LEVERAGE INEFFABLE HUMAN QUALITIES LIKE TRUST AND LOVE AS POWERFUL BUSINESS TOOLS THAT WOULD UNLOCK

PROSPERITY.

EVERYTHING WAS TIED UP IN **PROSPERITY THINKING**— THE BELIEF THAT WEALTH AND ABUNDANCE ARE NOT ONLY POSSIBLE BUT

DESERVED.

THE DEEPLY OPTIMISTIC, MATERIALISTIC, AND INDIVIDUALISTIC OUTLOOK IS SO ENMESHED IN AMERICAN CULTURE THAT THE AMWAY MODEL JUST SEEMED LIKE A **ROAD MAP** FOR ACHIEVING WHAT HAD BEEN **PROMISED ALL ALONG.**

ONCE NEW RECRUITS WERE IN, THEY WERE TAUGHT TO

"DREAM BUILD"

BY LOOKING TOWARD THEIR "UPLINES," THE PEOPLE
THERE BEFORE THEM, THE PEOPLE SO SUCCESSFUL
THEY HAD REACHED LEVELS OF SALES IDENTIFIED BY
PRECIOUS METALS AND JEWELS—SILVER AND GOLD,
PLATINUM AND RUBY, SAPPHIRE AND EMERALD,
DIAMOND AND CROWN.

AT CONFERENCES, UPLINES SHOWED OFF
THEIR FUR COATS AND FANCY CARS,
DISPLAYING THE DREAM IN REAL TIME,
ENCOURAGING THE SELLERS BELOW THEM
TO SELL MORE.

OVER THE YEARS SOME PEOPLE
MADE A LOT OF MONEY THROUGH AMWAY.
MANY MORE DIDN'T.

BECAUSE BAKED INTO
THE MLM MODEL IS THE
CORE PRINCIPLE THAT
IN ORDER FOR SOME
DIAMOND PEOPLE TO
GET VERY, VERY
RICH, A WHOLE LOT
OF OTHER PEOPLE
NEED TO BE MAKING
NEXT TO NOTHING
BELOW THEM.

A PYRAMID
NEEDS
ITS BASE.

MLMS AREN'T TECHNICALLY PYRAMID SCHEMES, BUT THE MODELS ARE SO SIMILAR THE FTC HAS A CONSUMER FACT SHEET TO HELP PEOPLE TELL THE TWO APART.

AND YET, THROUGH MILLIONS OF FAILURES, AND NUMEROUS LEGAL BATTLES, THE MLM MODEL HAS PERSEVERED, SEEING A SURGE OF POPULARITY IN THE 21ST CENTURY.

IN 2012, ANOTHER MLM FUSING RELIGION, SELF-EMPOWERMENT, PURPOSE, AND PROMISES OF A WEALTHY, SUCCESSFUL LIFESTYLE STARTED SHOWING UP ACROSS WOMEN'S FACEBOOK POSTS: LULAROE.

ITS WARES, LIKE AMWAY'S, WERE SIMPLE— THIS TIME, PATTERNED LEGGINGS INSTEAD OF LIQUID CLEANER— AND REVENUE SIMILARLY MUSHROOMED—FOUR YEARS AFTER ITS FOUNDING, THE COMPANY REPORTED $1 BILLION IN SALES.

ITS TENS OF THOUSANDS OF "DISTRIBUTORS," MAINLY YOUNG BLOND WHITE WOMEN, ATTEND CONVENTIONS AND CRUISES THAT ARE KNOWN TO HAVE THE FEELING AND FERVOR OF A RELIGIOUS REVIVAL—COFOUNDER MARK STIDHAM HAS COMPARED HIMSELF TO THE MORMON LEADER JOSEPH SMITH. AND SIMILAR TO AMWAY, THE COMPANY HAS BEEN MIRED IN CONTROVERSY— EX-MEMBERS HAVE DESCRIBED LULAROE AS BEING CULTLIKE AND SEXIST, AND IT HAS FACED NUMEROUS LAWSUITS.

WITH U.S. WAGES STAGNANT FOR DECADES,
AND THE COST OF LIVING AND EDUCATION

CLIMBING EVER UPWARD,

IT'S EASY TO SEE WHY THE DREAM MLMS PEDDLE,

THE POTENTIAL TO GET RICH QUICK,

HAS REMAINED AS INTOXICATING AS EVER.

THE MAJORITY OF MLM SELLERS ARE STILL THOUGHT

TO MAKE LESS THAN 70 CENTS AN HOUR.

IN FACT, A NUMBER OF STUDIES HAVE FOUND OVER

99 PERCENT OF ALL SELLERS MAKE NEXT TO NOTHING,

OR HAVE EVEN GONE INTO DEBT WORKING FOR AN MLM.

BUT SOMEONE IS GETTING RICH.

THE MLM INDUSTRY IS VALUED AT AROUND

$180 BILLION GLOBALLY.

WHEN HE DIED IN 2018, RICH DEVOS ALONE HAD
AMASSED A NET WORTH OF OVER $5 BILLION.

SO PRODUCTS CALLED SERENITY NOW AND

FREEDOM SLEEP AND 30 SECOND MIRACLE

KEEP TUMBLING DOWN THE LINE,
BECKONING FRIENDS TO USE ANYONE
AND EVERYONE THEY KNOW TO TRY TO MAKE

THE AMERICAN DREAM WORK.

NOSE TO THE GRINDSTONE

"I, TOO, LIVE IN THE TIME OF SLAVERY, BY WHICH I MEAN
I AM LIVING IN THE FUTURE CREATED BY IT."

—SAIDIYA V. HARTMAN

PECOS BILL WAS
RAISED BY COYOTES,
USED A RATTLESNAKE
NAMED SHAKE TO
LASSO TWISTERS,
AND ATE DYNAMITE.

PAUL BUNYAN WAS A COLOSSAL
LUMBERJACK WHO FELLED TREES IN A
SINGLE SWING, PALLED AROUND WITH A
GARGANTUAN BLUE OX NAMED BABE, AND
CREATED LAKES WITH HIS FOOTSTEPS.

AND JOHN HENRY WAS A POWERFUL
RAILROAD "STEEL-DRIVING MAN"
WHO WAS SO MIGHTY WITH
HIS HAMMER HE RACED A
STEAM DRILL TO SEE
WHO COULD TUNNEL
THROUGH ROCK
FASTER—AND

WON.

AMERICAN TALL TALES HAVE BEEN TAUGHT IN SCHOOLS FOR DECADES, GLORIFYING THE STRENGTH OF LARGER-THAN-LIFE MEN WHO TAMED **THE FRONTIER** AND BUILT OUR MODERN COUNTRY.

MOST OF THE CHARACTERS **ARE WHITE;** MOST ARE FICTIONAL.

BUT JOHN HENRY **IS BLACK,** AND HE WAS **REAL.**

AMERICAN VIEWS.

IN THE WAKE OF THE CIVIL WAR,
SOUTHERN STATES WERE DEEP IN DEBT,
AND CLAMORING FOR WAYS TO INCREASE REVENUE.

SO YOUNG, FREE BLACK MEN WERE ROUNDED UP
BY THE POLICE FOR IDLING, WALKING, TALKING,
AND JUST BEING, UNDER RESTRICTIVE, DISCRIMINATORY

"BLACK
CODES."

BACK THEN, THE ACCUSED HAD
TO PAY THEIR OWN COURT FEES.

SO BY THE TIME THE POLICE HAD FORCED THEM INTO JAIL
(WHICH THEY INVARIABLY DID)
THEY OWED THE STATE MONEY.

A STATE COULDN'T SQUEEZE REVENUE
OUT OF BLACK MEN BY
CLOTHING AND FEEDING
AND SHELTERING
THEM,

SO IT STARTED TO
LEASE THEM OUT
TO PRIVATE COMPANIES,
OFTEN TO MASSIVE RAILROAD COMPANIES, WHICH
WERE BOOMING AT THE TIME AND LOOKING FOR
CHEAP, EXPLOITABLE LABOR.

JOHN HENRY,
IT IS BELIEVED,
WAS ONE OF THOSE

"LEASED CONVICTS."

ACCOUNTS VARY,
BUT THE MOST
WIDELY CITED
CLAIMS THAT IN
1866, AN EIGHTEEN-YEAR-OLD
JOHN HENRY WAS WORKING FOR THE UNION
ARMY WHEN HE WAS ARRESTED FOR ALLEGEDLY STEALING
FOOD FROM A GROCERY STORE. AFTER A (LIKELY UNFAIR) TRIAL,
HE WAS SENTENCED TO TEN YEARS IN PRISON
AT THE VIRGINIA STATE PENITENTIARY.

THE PENITENTIARY TURNED AROUND AND LEASED HIM TO THE

CHESAPEAKE AND OHIO RAILROAD—C&O—

WHICH PAID HIM TWENTY-FIVE CENTS A DAY FOR HARD LABOR.

JOHN HENRY WAS, INDEED, MASTERFUL WITH HIS HAMMER.

BUT HE ALMOST CERTAINLY DIDN'T DIE RACING A STEAM DRILL.

IN ALL LIKELIHOOD HE DIED THE WAY HUNDREDS
UPON HUNDREDS OF OTHER LEASED PRISONERS DID—

FROM BEING FORCED TO WORK IN BRUTAL,
INHUMANE CONDITIONS, BREATHING IN
SILICA DUST UNTIL HE CHOKED.

CONVICT LEASING WAS
WILDLY PROFITABLE
FOR RAILROAD COMPANIES LIKE C&O.

IT ALSO BROUGHT
A WINDFALL
FOR THE STATES
IMPRISONING AND
LEASING THEIR
CITIZENS OUT.

ALABAMA, FOR ONE,
MADE $1 MILLION
($26 MILLION TODAY)
OFF PRISON MINES
IN 1912 ALONE.

ALABAMA WAS THE LAST STATE TO
END CONVICT LEASING IN 1928,
BUT TODAY, PRISONS STILL
**RELY ON EXPLOITING
THE LABOR OF THE
PEOPLE THEY IMPRISON.**
INCARCERATED FIREFIGHTERS IN
CALIFORNIA, FOR EXAMPLE, MAKE $1
AN HOUR FIGHTING INCREASINGLY INTENSE
CLIMATE-CHANGE-FUELED BLAZES.

THE IMPRISONED ARE,
DISPROPORTIONATELY,
BLACK MEN.

AFTER JOHN HENRY DIED, LABORERS BEGAN TO SING
A BLUES BALLAD ABOUT THE FOLK HERO'S LIFE—

"THE BALLAD OF JOHN HENRY."

THE SONG WAS FIRST USED BY CREWS TO

STEADY AND SYNCHRONIZE
THEIR LABOR,

AND OVER THE YEARS IT MORPHED
INTO THE MOST RECORDED FOLK
SONG EVER, WITH DOZENS OF
VARIATIONS AND HUNDREDS
OF VERSES.

IN THE 1980S, SHERMAN JAMES, A BLACK EPIDEMIOLOGIST,
COINED THE TERM "JOHN HENRYISM"
TO DESCRIBE THE BELIEF HELD BY SOME BLACK PEOPLE
(ESPECIALLY POOR AND WORKING-CLASS PEOPLE WHO
LIVE IN HIGHLY SEGREGATED AREAS)
THAT IF THEY WORK HARD ENOUGH,
IF THEY PUT IN SOME COLOSSAL MENTAL AND
PHYSICAL COMMITMENT, THEY WILL BE ABLE TO
CONTROL THEIR ENVIRONMENT
AND OVERCOME THE CORROSIVE EFFECTS OF
CENTURIES OF STRUCTURAL RACISM.

HE FOUND,
AS WAS THE CASE
WITH JOHN HENRY,
THAT EXERTION
CAN INCREASE THE
RISK OF AN
UNTIMELY
DEATH.

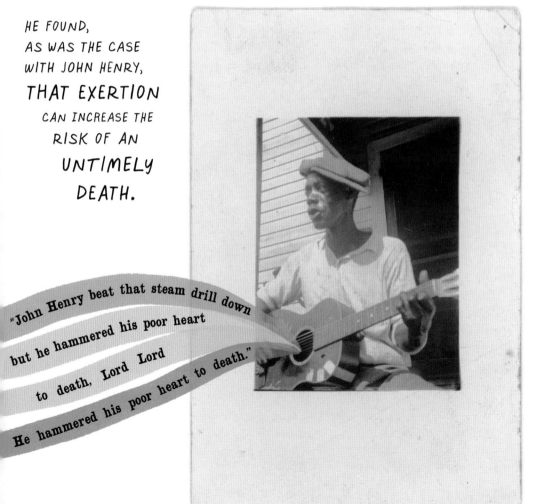

"John Henry beat that steam drill down
but he hammered his poor heart
to death, Lord Lord
He hammered his poor heart to death."

WE THE PEOPLE

"WE ARE THE ONES WE HAVE BEEN WAITING FOR."

—JUNE JORDAN

ON A SWELTERING SUNDAY IN JULY OF 1969, NEIGHBORS AROUND **EL BARRIO—** THE PREDOMINANTLY PUERTO RICAN NEIGHBORHOOD OF NEW YORK CITY— LOOKED OUT THEIR WINDOWS AND SAW HIGH SCHOOL AND COLLEGE KIDS **SWEEPING UP TRASH.**

ONE WAY

OVERFLOWING TRASH FESTERING ON THE SIDEWALKS AND IN THE STREETS WAS A CONSTANT PROBLEM IN EL BARRIO BECAUSE, NO MATTER HOW MANY TIMES PEOPLE COMPLAINED, SANITATION TRUCKS WOULDN'T VISIT THE AREA NEARLY AS OFTEN AS THEY DID **THE WHITE NEIGHBORHOODS.**

NEIGHBORS WERE CONFUSED, AND WATCHED FROM A DISTANCE. BUT WHEN THE KIDS WERE BACK THE NEXT SUNDAY, AND THE SUNDAY AFTER THAT, PEOPLE STARTED COMING DOWN

THE TEENS WERE PART OF A BUDDING GROUP CALLED THE YOUNG LORDS.

MODELED AFTER THE BLACK PANTHER PARTY, THEY WERE LOOKING FOR WAYS TO SERVE THEIR COMMUNITY WHILE DRAWING ATTENTION TO **SYSTEMIC INJUSTICES.**

GARBAGE WAS THE PERFECT FIRST ACTION, BECAUSE IT WAS HIGHLY VISIBLE, A HUGE PROBLEM, AND THEY KNEW THEY COULD **MAKE AN IMMEDIATE DIFFERENCE.**

NEIGHBORS CAME OUT TO HELP, SO THE YOUNG LORDS WENT TO THE SANITATION DEPARTMENT TO ASK FOR MORE BROOMS. THE CITY REFUSED TO GIVE THEM THE BROOMS, BUT THE YOUNG LORDS TOOK THEM ANYWAY

AND SWEPT ALL THE GARBAGE—

TRASH CANS, ABANDONED CARS, RUSTING APPLIANCES—INTO THE MIDDLE OF SEVERAL MAJOR INTERSECTIONS,

AND SET IT ON FIRE.

IT WAS REFERRED TO AS **"THE GARBAGE OFFENSIVE."**

TRAFFIC WAS BLOCKED, THE MEDIA COVERED IT, AND THE CITY WAS FINALLY FORCED TO **CLEAN IT ALL UP.**

YOUNG

THE YOUNG LORDS WERE ENERGIZED AND CONTINUED TO FOCUS ON PRACTICAL WAYS TO "SERVE THE PEOPLE" BY FILLING GAPS WHERE THE GOVERNMENT WAS FAILING THEIR COMMUNITY—

HEALTH
FOOD
EDUCATION
HOUSING.

WORKING PARENTS DIDN'T HAVE ACCESS TO AFFORDABLE CHILDCARE, SO THE YOUNG LORDS OCCUPIED CHURCHES AND

RAN FREE BREAKFAST PROGRAMS AND FREE DAYCARES.

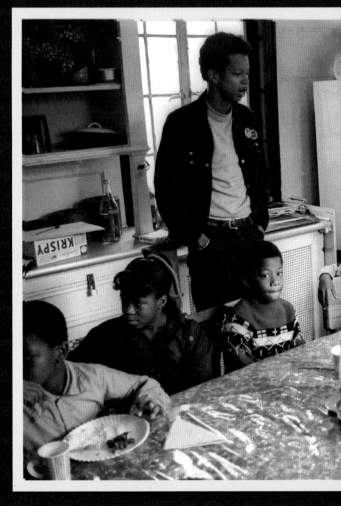

MANY DIDN'T HAVE ACCESS TO QUALITY HEALTHCARE, INCLUDING THE LEAD POISONING AND TUBERCULOSIS TESTS OTHER NEW YORKERS HAD, SO THE YOUNG LORDS ADMINISTERED DOOR-TO-DOOR LEAD TESTING THEMSELVES, AND COMMANDEERED A CITY-OWNED TB-TESTING X-RAY TRUCK TO PROVIDE FREE SCREENINGS.

LORDS

NYC PUBLIC SCHOOLS WHITEWASHED PUERTO RICAN HISTORY, SO THE YOUNG LORDS TAUGHT KIDS ABOUT WHERE THEY CAME FROM THROUGH POETRY. THEY CONNECTED CONTEMPORARY STRUGGLES FOR LIBERATION TO CENTURIES OF RESISTANCE— THE TAÍNOS RESISTING SPANISH COLONIZATION IN THE 16TH CENTURY, AND DON PEDRO ALBIZU CAMPOS RESISTING U.S. IMPERIALISM IN THE MID-20TH CENTURY.

WHEN THEY SAW PEOPLE SUFFERING FROM DRUG ADDICTION, THEY DEVELOPED INNOVATIVE DRUG-REHABILITATION PROGRAMS. WHEN THEY SAW THE LOCAL HOSPITAL PROVIDING MURDEROUSLY INADEQUATE CARE, THEY OCCUPIED IT, AND **DEMANDED BETTER.**

YOUNG LORDS MEMBERSHIP GREW INTO THE THOUSANDS BEFORE IT DISBANDED IN 1976, BUT LIKE OTHER REVOLUTIONARY CIVIL RIGHTS ORGANIZATIONS OF THAT ERA—THE BLACK PANTHERS, BROWN BERETS, I WOR KUEN, THE AMERICAN INDIAN MOVEMENT— THE YOUNG LORDS HAD A **MASSIVE IMPACT** ON ONGOING IDENTITY AND ACTIVISM.

IN THE U.S. THERE IS A RICH HISTORY OF MARGINALIZED GROUPS COMING TOGETHER TO SUPPORT ONE ANOTHER IN THE FACE OF SYSTEMIC RACISM AND NEGLECT, OFTEN FOCUSING ON THE

THE SAME ISSUES THE YOUNG LORDS DID:

FROM PRE-CONTACT UNTIL TODAY,
THE CHEROKEE TRADITION OF GADUGI
HAS CALLED PEOPLE TO WORK TOGETHER AND HELP ONE ANOTHER.

IN THE 18TH CENTURY,
THE FREE AFRICAN SOCIETY
CARED FOR PHILADELPHIA'S BLACK (AND WHITE) RESIDENTS DURING THE BRUTAL 1793 YELLOW FEVER EPIDEMIC.

THROUGHOUT THE 19TH CENTURY,
BLACK WOMEN DROVE MUTUAL AID EFFORTS
DOING EVERYTHING FROM ESTABLISHING DAYCARES TO NIGHT SCHOOLS TO SCHOLARSHIP FUNDS.

IN THE EARLY 20TH CENTURY,
IMMIGRANT COMMUNITIES
FORMED ORGANIZATIONS LIKE THE CHINESE CONSOLIDATED BENEVOLENT ASSOCIATION, JEWISH LANDSMANSHAFTN, AND SOCIADES MUTUALISTAS, TO HELP NEW ARRIVALS GET SITUATED, POOL POWER, AND PROTECT WORKERS.

IN THE LATE 20TH CENTURY,
THE QUEER COMMUNITY
BANDED TOGETHER TO FORM NETWORKS OF CARE DURING
THE AIDS CRISIS LIKE THE CHICKEN SOUP BRIGADE.

TODAY, AS MANY STRUGGLE TO SECURE ACCESS TO AFFORDABLE
HEALTHCARE, HOUSING, EDUCATION, AND FOOD, MUTUAL AID EFFORTS—
FROM COMMUNITY FRIDGES TO LEGAL AID—CONTINUE TO SURGE.

"... A MOVEMENT BEGINS WITH ONE PERSON REACHING OUT TO JOIN WITH ONE OTHER,"

WROTE IRIS MORALES AND DENISE OLIVER-VELEZ;
TWO OF THE LEADERS OF THE YOUNG LORDS.

"THE YOUNG LORDS
STARTED WITH ONLY
A HANDFUL
OF US, SOME OF
US NO OLDER
THAN
FIFTEEN."

"WE STILL
IN THE POWER
PEOPLE TO
THE WORLD."

BELIEVE
OF YOUNG
CHANGE

—IRIS MORALES AND
DENISE OLIVER-VELEZ
The Young Lords: A Reader
2010

AFTERWORD

In Arroyo Hondo, New Mexico, there is an ancient petroglyph carved into high red rock that shows a giant with a labyrinth for a head sitting next to a person on a horse. No one has been able to date it, but it's thought to have been carved by different people over the span of hundreds if not thousands of years. The labyrinth giant is most likely ancient, with the horse added in later, after the Spanish arrived 500 years ago.

Images of ancient labyrinths have been found etched into rocks all over the world, from the United Kingdom to Greece to Peru. In the United States there are many, especially across the southwest in places like Arizona, Utah, and Nevada. A labyrinth is carved high up on a wall in Casa Grande, built by the Salado people in the early 1300s. Another is chiseled in a lower room of Montezuma Castle, cliff dwellings built by Sinagua people in the 1100s. More are sculpted into the Tonto National Monument and Minnie's Gap and Winnemucca Lake.

Labyrinths aren't just found as petroglyphs; they've made their way into all sorts of objects and artifacts. The Hopi consider the labyrinth to be a sacred symbol, and labyrinths appear often in Hopi baskets and silverwork.

Unlike other ancient symbols, labyrinths also exist at human scale as stone paths and tile designs on the ground. It's a symbol you can physically enter and walk through.

People often use the words *labyrinth* and *maze* interchangeably, but they are very different things.

While a maze is intentionally confusing, designed to get you lost, a labyrinth is the opposite. A labyrinth is a path that leads you on a journey. Walking one is supposed to allow you time to reflect and to contemplate.

Labyrinths lead you to the heart of something, and then back out again. A labyrinth's circuits fold in on themselves, so that as you walk, you see where you've been, and where you will go. The path doesn't change, but your relationship to it does. With every turn, every doubling back, where you've been and where you are going are seen in a new light. Your perception of the path grows and deepens as you go.

We can't change the past. But we can live in relationship with it in a way that informs and energizes our present. We are walking through history all the time, and it is up to us to keep circling, to keep engaging, to keep

REACHING
FOR THE
HEART OF
THINGS.

ACKNOWLEDGMENTS

This book would not exist without the people whose stories these are—everyone both named and unnamed who has fought and dreamed and pushed for a better, more just world. Your lives and voices and work inspire me every single day.

I am forever indebted to the historians, archivists, photographers, and artists whose work I've built on here. These stories and images have long been in circulation, and I really see my role as collecting them and collaging them into a new form. If you're interested in a particular history, I urge you to keep digging and read/watch/listen to the works listed in the selected bibliography here, as well as access a slew of other resources (written and visual) on the website: www.americareduxbook.com. (To every person who has uploaded a public domain image in hi-res and tagged it specifically, I am absolutely in love with you and squealed with delight every time I found your file.)

Thank you to my agent, Jenny Stephens, for reaching out to me and asking if I had a book in me—turns out I did, and you changed my life. Thank you to my editor, Donna Bray, for believing in this book and letting me run wild—in breadth, in format, in vision. Your support means so much, and the second you were interested I knew Balzer + Bray was meant to be this book's home. Thank you to everyone at HarperCollins, especially Chris Kwon, Jenna Stempel-Lobell, and Alison Donalty, for dealing with such a weird little book and figuring out how to get it made.

To my expert readers, including Janna Haider, Katrina Phillips, and Rachel Pitkin, thank you for offering up your minds, your insight, your guidance. Your feedback was invaluable.

Thank you to all the people who said yes to my visual stories before I even knew what they were and allowed me to explore and play them into existence—John Borthwick, Khoi Vinh, David Jacobs, Blake Eskin, Geoff Kelly, Mark Byrnes—I wouldn't have been able to get to this point without you.

Thank you to CityLab for being such an incredible advocate of my work, and for being the home where earlier versions of some of these stories took root. You guys are the best.

A HUGE thank you to everyone who is thinking out loud and has allowed me into those spaces and conversations, whether it be dear friends on Marco (hi, Talia) or strangers whose social feeds have made me infinitely smarter (Kaitlyn Greenidge, Chanda Prescod-Weinstein, Bree Newsome, Kelly Hayes, Eve L. Ewing) or absolutely incredible, generous thinkers I've followed and then had the honor of collaborating with (Mariame Kaba). These conversations are everything to me. A model for how to think and be and create in the world.

Thank you to all the artists who have inspired me, especially fellow visual storytellers, for creating expansive visual spaces that upend genres and ways of seeing. To Lauren Redniss for showing me an entire form; *Radioactive* made me understand the book I someday wanted to create. To Wendy MacNaughton for encouraging me and believing in my work. To Mira Jacob (and everyone in my Tin House crew!) for including me, and seeing me, and offering advice about this book.

To NYSCA/NYFA for recognizing my work. Your support both let me know I was on the right track and gave me the financial assistance I needed to get the job done. To Casey Scieszka and Steven Weinberg for accepting me into my very first residency at Spruceton Inn and gifting me space. To JillEllyn Riley for supporting me and cheering me on and being so graceful with guidance always.

To all of the educators and librarians and young people I have had the pleasure of working with since this book came out. Coming into your schools and classrooms, watching the ways you are lighting up your brains and hearts to make sense of this world and including this book in those conversations—nothing brings me more joy!

To Jill and Kristie and Candie and Ella and Molly and all the others who cared for my tiny humans so that I could work. Without childcare, this book would not exist.

To my dad for showing me how art can be work and how it's both a calling and a duty. To my mom for the wonder and the fire, all the fire.

And to Inbal, my wonderful Inbal. The beginning of this form started in those journals I was keeping when you found me in Barcelona so many years ago. How happy I am that you found me, and that we've made this life together, these humans together. You, Daniel, and Roane are my entire world. I love you.

IMAGE SOURCES

Nearly all the images in this book are in the public domain, collected from archives such as the Library of Congress, the New York Public Library, the National Archives, the Smithsonian, HathiTrust, and others. You can find a visual database of every single image in the book listed with descriptions, creators, and links back to original sources at www.americareduxbook.com. The following images are exceptions and have been licensed to use.

SELECTED BIBLIOGRAPHY

Chapter 1: The Good Old Days

I first learned about the United Daughters of the Confederacy via Dr. Karen L. Cox, who wrote the definitive book on the group and their work:

Cox, Karen L. *Dixie's Daughters: The United Daughters of the Confederacy and the Preservation of Confederate Culture.* University Press of Florida, 2019.

This is a great short video that features Dr. Cox and talks about the UDC's efforts to create both physical and living monuments (and has examples from other textbooks):

Vox Editors. "How Southern Socialites Rewrote Civil War History." 25 Oct. 2017, https://www.youtube.com/watch?v=dOkFXPblLpU

For more about the campaigns to get teachers fired and how the UDC's work led to school segregation read:

Huffman, Greg. "Twisted Sources: How Confederate Propaganda Ended Up in the South's Schoolbooks." Facing South, 10 Apr. 2019, https://www.facingsouth.org/2019/04/twistedsources-How-confederate-propaganda-ended-souths-schoolbooks

And these academic papers contributed greatly to details included in this chapter:

Bailey, Fred Arthur. "The Textbooks of the 'Lost Cause': Censorship and the Creation of Southern State Histories." *Georgia Historical Quarterly*, vol. 75, no. 3, 1991, pp. 507–33, http://www.jstor.org/stable/40582363

Greenhouse, Steven. "'The point is intimidation': Florida teachers besieged by draconian laws." *The Guardian*, 13 May 2023, https://www.theguardian.com/us-news/2023/may/13/florida-teachers-woke-law-ron-desantis

Johnson, Joan Marie. "'Drill into us . . . the Rebel Tradition': The Contest over Southern Identity in Black and White Women's Clubs, South Carolina, 1898–1930." *Journal of Southern History*, vol. 66, no. 3, 2000, pp. 525–62, https://www.jstor.org/stable/2587867?seq=1education/2023/03/06/slavery-was-wrong-5-other-things-educators-wont-teach-anymore/

Zimmerman, Jonathan. "Brown-Ing the American Textbook: History, Psychology, and the Origins of Modern Multiculturalism." *History of Education Quarterly*, vol. 44, no. 1, 2004, pp. 46–69, http://www.jstor.org/stable/3218110

And these are the sources for contemporary censorship:

Aberg-Riger, Ariel. "The Fight for the American Public Library." Bloomberg, 26 Apr. 2023, https://www.bloomberg.com/news/features/2023-04-26/how-to-protect-your-local-library-from-book-ban-campaigns

Hawkins, Alicia. "Lawmakers introduced 563 measures against critical race theory in 2021 and 2022." Newsroom UCLA, 6 Apr. 2023, https://newsroom.ucla.edu/releases/lawmakers-introduced-measures-against-critical-race-theory#:~:text=A%20UCLA%20Law%20study%20found,those%20measures%20have%20been%20adopted

Natanson, Hannah. "'Slavery was wrong' and 5 other things some educators won't teach anymore." *The Washington Post*, 6 Mar. 2023, https://www.washingtonpost.com/

Go online to view some wild primary sources, like full pages from the Alabama textbook *Know Alabama.*

Chapter 2: Let Freedom Ring

This piece by Dr. Manisha Sinha about slave resistance being central to the abolitionist movement was a huge influence on this chapter:

Sinha, Manisha. "Slave Resistance" from *The Slave's Cause: A History of Abolition*, Yale University Press, 2016, pp. 381–420, https://humilityandconviction.uconn.edu/wp-content/uploads/sites/1877/2019/02/Sinha-Slave-Resistance.pdf

Specific statistics like "producing more cotton on those stolen lands than all the other countries in the world combined" (p. 23) and "more than all the capital invested in railroads and factories combined" (p. 32) come from the following two sources, respectively:

Stephenson, Frank. "Dixie, Debunked: Historian Paints a Global, Modern View of the Old South and Origins of the Civil War." Review of *The Fragile Fabric of Union: Cotton, Federal Politics, and the Global Origins of the Civil War,* by Brian Schoen. Ohio Research Communications, 1 Jan. 2012, https://www.ohio.edu/research/communications/dixie

Johnson, Walter. "King Cotton's Long Shadow." *New York Times*, 30 Mar. 2013, https://opinionator.blogs.nytimes.com/2013/03/30/king-cottons-long-shadow/

I love exploring history visually through exhibitions, and this one influenced this chapter:

Subversion & The Art of Slavery. 12 Mar. 2021–22 Jan. 2022, Schomburg Center for Research in Black Culture, New York Public Library, New York, https://www.nypl.org/events/exhibitions/Subversion-art-slavery-abolition

And Mariame Kaba is a modern-day abolitionist whose work inspires me and who first introduced me to figures like David Ruggles:

Kaba, Mariame. "Yes, We Mean Literally Abolish the Police: Because Reform Won't Happen." *New York Times*, 12 Jun. 2020, https://www.nytimes.com/2020/06/12/opinion/sunday/floydabolish-defund-police.html

Chapter 3: Spreading Democracy

This great piece by Dina Gilio-Whitaker (Colville Confederated Tribes) inspired and grounded the framing for this chapter:

Gilio-Whitaker, Dina. "The Indigenous Roots of Modern Feminism." *Beacon Broadside*, 11 Mar. 2020, https://www.beaconbroadside.com/broadside/2020/03/the-indigenous-roots-of-modern-feminism.html

Gilio-Whitaker references Dr. Sally Roesch Wagner's work, which I also drew upon:

Wagner, Sally Roesch. "How Native American Women Inspired the Women's Rights Movement." National Park Service, https://www.nps.gov/articles/000/how-native-american-women-inspired-the-women-s-rights-movement.htm

There are scores of incredible books written about the history of feminism and the women's rights movement. Three that contributed to the making of this chapter include:

Beck, Koa. *White Feminism: From the Suffragettes to Influencers and Who They Leave Behind.* Atria Books, 2021.

Davis, Angela. *Women, Race & Class.* Vintage Books, 1983.

Jones, Martha S. *Vanguard: How Black Women Broke Barriers, Won the Vote, and Insisted on Equality for All.* Basic Books, 2020.

Finally, I learned more about #cripthevote and statistics about disability turnout from the following sources (and from following Alice Wong on Twitter @SFdirewolf):

Kim, Sara. "Crip the Vote Hashtag Brings Attention to People with Disabilities." *Teen Vogue*, 27 Oct. 2016, https://www.teenvogue.com/story/crip-the-vote-hashtag-persons-with-disabilities-election-campaign

Schur, Lisa, and Douglas Kruse. "Fact Sheet: Disability and Voter Turnout in the 2020 Elections." Rutgers and the U.S. Election Assistance Commission, 2020, https://www.eac.gov/sites/default/files/document_library/files/Fact_sheet_on_disability_and_voter_turnout_in_2020_0.pdf

Go online to browse more images and a great Library of Congress exhibit.

Chapter 4: A Nation of Immigrants

I drew from this interview with Jia Lynn Yang, author of *One Mighty and Irresistible Tide*, which gives a good overview of the arc of restrictionist immigration measures:

Diamond, Anna. "The 1924 Law That Slammed the Door on Immigrants and the Politicians Who Pushed It Back Open." Review of *One Mighty and Irresistible Tide: The Epic Struggle Over American Immigration 1924–1965*, by Jia Lynn. *Smithsonian Magazine*, 19 May 2020, https:// www.smithsonianmag.com/history/1924-law-slammed-door-immigrants-and-politicians-who-pushed-it-back-open-180974910/

As does this piece:

Fontes, Anthony W. "The Long, Bipartisan History of Dealing with Immigrants Harshly." *The Chicago Reporter*, 11 Jul. 2019, https://www.chicagoreporter.com/the-long-bipartisan-history-of-dealing-with-immigrants-harshly/

I learned about President Harding's celebrity support from this article:

Giaimo, Cara. "Warren G. Harding Was the First Celebrity-Endorsed President." Atlas Obscura, 31 Aug. 2015, https://www.atlasobscura.com/articles/warren-g-harding-was-the-first-celebrityendorsed-president

And more about Lillian Russell's specific influence through a number of newspaper articles from the time, including this one (you can see links to many more, including ridiculously juicy celebrity profiles online):

"Senate 'Gallants' Clash: Lillian Russell as Immigration Expert, Caused Debate." *Kansas City Star*, 16 Apr. 1922, https://www.newspapers.com/image/654235017/

Press coverage from the time about the passage of the 1924 Johnson-Reed Act is stunning:

Reed, David A. "America of the Melting Pot Comes to End." *New York Times*, 27 Apr. 1924, https://timesmachine.nytimes.com/timesmachine/1924/04/27/101592734.html?pageNumber=181

This entry provided context about US immigration law vis–à–vis the Holocaust:

"United States Immigration and Refugee Law, 1921–1980." *Holocaust Encyclopedia*, United States Holocaust Memorial Museum, https://encyclopedia.ushmm.org/content/en/article/unitedstates-immigration-and-refugee-law-1921-1980

And background about the US-Mexican border came from this piece:

Massey, Douglas S. "The Mexico-U.S. Border in the American Imagination." *Proceedings of the American Philosophical Society*, vol. 160, no. 2, 2016, pp. 160–77, http://www.jstor.org/stable/26159208

Chapter 5: Traditional Family Values

Films, TV shows, and interactive exhibits really helped me get my arms around this chapter,

including:

Eugenic Rubicon: California's Sterilization Stories. Arizona State and University of Michigan. Edited by Jacqueline Wernimont and Alexandra Minna Stern, 2017, https://scalar.usc.edu/works/eugenic-rubicon-/index

The Eugenics Crusade: What's Wrong with Perfect? Edited by George O'Donnell, PBS, 2018.

No Más Bebés. Produced and Directed by Renee Tajima-Peña, PBS, 2016.

This three-part series is a good overview about eugenics in the US after World War II:

Begos, Kevin. "The American Eugenics Movement After World War II." *Indy Week*, 18 May 2011, https://indyweek.com/news/american-eugenics-movement-world-war-ii-part-1-3/

Newspaper clippings from the time were essential in getting a sense of what the Fitter Families contests were like (you can see more online):

"Human Pedigrees Like the Cattle: The State of Kansas Opens a Family Registry Department to Give Prizes and Put on Record Your Inherited Good Points, Just Like the Prize Hen, Fattest Hog, Wooliest Sheep, and Cow That Gives the Most Milk." *Fort Worth Record*, 3 Aug. 1924, https://www.newspapers.com/image/637832123

The following academic articles contributed greatly to my research (and go into much more detail if you want to keep reading):

Torpy, Sally J. "Native American Women and Coerced Sterilization: On the Trail of Tears in the 1970s." *American Indian Culture and Research Journal*, vol. 24, no. 2, 2000, pp. 1–22, https://www.law.berkeley.edu/php-programs/centers/crrj/zotero/loadfile.php?entity_key=QFDB5MW3

Lawrence, Jane. "The Indian Health Service and the Sterilization of Native American Women." *American Indian Quarterly*, vol. 24, no. 3, 2000, pp. 400–19, http://www.jstor.org/stable/1185911

Mass, Bonnie. "Puerto Rico: A Case Study of Population Control." *Latin American Perspectives*, vol. 4, no. 4, 1977, pp. 66–81, http://www.jstor.org/stable/2633177

Go online to see more links to articles, including recent press about the involuntary sterilization of disabled people.

Chapter 6: One Nation Under God

This is the piece that first introduced me to the connection between anti-abortion and pro-segregation movements:

Balmer, Randall. "The Real Origins of the Religious Right: They'll Tell You it was Abortion. Sorry, The Historical Record's Clear: It Was Segregation." *Politico Magazine*, 27 May 2014, https://www.politico.com/magazine/story/2014/05/religious-right-real-origins-107133/

If you're more of a visual learner, this video contributed to my research, as did the associated article:

How Segregation Influenced Evangelical Political Activism. Produced by Shawn Hamilton, Sandra McDaniel, and Scott Michels, Retro Report, 2018.

Haberman, Clyde. "Religion and Right-Wing Politics: How Evangelicals Reshaped Elections." *New York Times*, 28 Oct. 2018, https://www.nytimes.com/2018/10/28/us/religion-politicsevangelicals.html

For deep dives into Jerry Falwell and the Moral Majority, the following pieces provide background and insight:

Banwart, Doug. "Jerry Falwell, the Rise of the Moral Majority, and the 1980 Election." *Western Illinois Historical Review*, vol. V, Spring 2013, http://www.wiu.edu/cas/history/wihr/pdfs/Banwart-MoralMajorityVol5.pdf

Blumenthal, Max. "Agent of Intolerance." *Nation*, 16 May 2007, https://www.thenation.com/article/archive/agent-intolerance/

FitzGerald, Frances. "A Disciplined, Charging Army." *New Yorker*, 18 May 1981, https://www.newyorker.com/magazine/1981/05/18/a-disciplined-charging-army

And this piece connects the legacy of the Moral Majority to Donald Trump:

Prothero, Stephen. "When Donald Trump Goes to Liberty U." CNN, 17 Jan. 2016, https://edition.cnn.com/2016/01/16/opinions/prothero-trump-liberty/index.html

Go online for more newspaper articles about the I Love America rallies, and to see archives of the *Moral Majority Report*.

Chapter 7: Home of the Brave

I found documentaries and oral histories to be invaluable to the research of this chapter. They give such an incredible sense of the power of ACT UP's organizing and spirited collective action:

ACT UP Albany Action. Directed by Jim Hubbard, Jim Hubbard Films, 1988, https://www.jimhubbardfilms.com/unedited-footage/act-up-albany-action-1988

ACT UP Oral History Project, https://actuporalhistory.org/

Fight Back, Fight AIDS. Directed by James Wentzy, Frameline Distribution, 2014, https://vimeo.com/ondemand/fightbackfightaids

How to Survive a Plague. Directed by David France, Sundance Selects, 2012

United in Anger: A History of ACT UP. Directed by Jim Hubbard, 2012, https://vimeo.com/ondemand/unitedinangerjh

I also relied on Sarah Schulman's incredibly detailed history of ACT UP:

Schulman, Sarah. *Let the Record Show: A Political History of ACT UP New York, 1987–1993*. Farrar, Straus and Giroux, 2021.

This dissertation also provided details about women in the movement, like Katrina Haslip, who are often overlooked in accounts of ACT UP's work:

Hedger, Kathryn. *Standing Against a "Willful and Deadly Negligence" The Development of a Feminist Response to the AIDS Crisis*. 2018. Texas State University, MA dissertation. https://digital.library.txstate.edu/bitstream/handle/10877/7467/HEDGER-THESIS-2018.pdf

Go online to see the AIDS issue of the Moral Majority Report referenced at the beginning of the chapter, as well as a number of newspaper articles from the time.

Chapter 8: Give Me Liberty

I was inspired to write this chapter after listening to this podcast

"American Shadows." *Throughline*, hosted by Rund Abdelfatah and Ramtin Arablouei, NPR, 7 Mar. 2019, https://www.npr.org/transcripts/694463513?storyId=694463513%3FstoryId%3D694463513

If you want to read the original *Journal of Occurrences* in its entirety:

Dickerson, Oliver Morton. *Boston Under Military Rule 1768–1769 As Revealed In A Journal of the Times*. Chapman & Grimes Mount Vernon Press, 1936, https://hdl.handle.net/2027/mdp.39015008570163

Other articles that contributed to my research and offered perspective on the role of propaganda and conspiracy theories in American history:

Hünemörder, Markus. "American Revolution." *Conspiracy Theories in American History: An Encyclopedia, Volume 1*, ABC CLIO, 2003, pp. 59–61

Kazin, Michael. "The Paranoid Streak in American History." *Los Angeles Times*, 27 Oct. 1996, https://www.latimes.com/archives/la-xpm-1996-10-27-op-58345-story.html

Standerfer, Amanda. "An Organized Incident: The Boston Massacre Re-Examined." *Historia, Eastern Illinois University History Department Journal*, vol. V, 1995–96, https://www.eiu.edu/historia/Standerfer.pdf

Thum, Gladys, and Marcella Thum. "War Propaganda and the American Revolution: The Pen and the Sword." *Readings in Propaganda and Persuasion: New and Classic Essays*, edited by Garth Jowett and Victoria O'Donnell, Sage, 2006, pp. 73–82

Winston, Alexander. "Firebrand of the Revolution." *American Heritage*, vol. 18, no. 3, April 1967, https://www.americanheritage.com/firebrand-revolution#

Chapter 9: Good Guy with a Gun

Books about Sam Colt's life and work:

Hosley, William. *Colt: The Making of an American Legend*. University of Massachusetts, 1996.

Houze, Herbert G. *Samuel Colt: Arms, Art, and Invention*. Yale University Press, 2006.

Kelly, Jack. *The Invention of the Revolver: The Saga of Sam Colt*. Kindle Edition, 2010.

The statistic "Colt firearms became the first truly global manufacturing export in American history" (p. 113) is from this exhibit:

The Colt Revolver in the American West. Ongoing, Autry Museum of the American West, Los Angeles. Online catalog: https://web.archive.org/web/20120421032356/http://theautry.org/thecolt-revolver-in-the-american-west/overview

Articles that added perspective and context about American gun culture include:

Hix, Lisa. "Why Americans Love Guns." *Collectors Weekly*, 2 Oct. 2013, https://www.collectorsweekly.com/articles/why-americans-love-guns/

Onion, Rebecca. "Automatic for the People." *Topic*, Jul. 2018, https://www.topic.com/automatic-for-the-people

Bellesiles, Michael A. "The Origins of Gun Culture in the United States, 1760–1865." *Journal of American History*, vol. 83, no. 2, September 1996, p. 428, https://www.jstor.org/stable/2944942

Chapter 10: A New World

I first learned of Mustafa Al-Azemmouri from this piece:

Haselby, Sam. "Muslims of Early America." *Aeon*, https://aeon.co/essays/muslims-lived-in-america-before-protestantism-even-existed

If you're fascinated by this abbreviated retelling, you can read the full 1555 story:

de Vaca, Cabeza. *La Relación (1555 Edition)*. The Wittliff Collections, Texas State University, https://exhibits.library.txstate.edu/cabeza/exhibits/show/cabeza-de-vaca/relacion

The following academic papers were critical in providing insight into Al-Azemmouri's

historical significance and legacy:

Adorno, Rolena. "Estevanico's Legacy: Insights into Colonial Latin American Studies." *Journal of Iberian and Latin American Literacy and Cultural Studies*, vol. 1, no. 2, 2001, https://arachne.libraries.rutgers.edu/index.php/arachne/article/view/13/25

Chaouch, Khalid. "Claiming Estevanico de Azamor in the Labyrinth of Oriental/Western Identities." *Middle Ground Journal of Literary and Cultural Encounters*, issue 6, 2014, https://www.academia.edu/35102097/Claiming_Estevanico_de_Azamor_in_the_Labyrinth_of_Oriental_Western_Identities

McDonald, Dedra S. "Intimacy and Empire: Indian-African Interaction in Spanish Colonial New Mexico, 1500-1800." *American Indian Quarterly*, vol. 22, no. 1/2, 1998, pp. 134–56, http://www.jstor.org/stable/1185114

Sánchez, Ramón. "Slavery and captivity in Álvar Núñez Cabeza de Vaca's 1542 La Relación." *Corpus*, vol. 6, no. 2, July/December 2016, https://journals.openedition.org/corpusarchivos/1682

Simour, Lhoussain. "(De)slaving history: Mostafa al-Azemmouri, the sixteenth-century Moroccan captive in the tale of conquest." *European Review of History*, vol. 20, no. 3 May 2013, https://www.tandfonline.com/doi/abs/10.1080/13507486.2012.745830

As were these nonacademic pieces:

Solnit, Rebecca. "Crossing Over." *Paris Review*, 20 Mar. 2018, https://www.theparisreview.org/blog/2018/03/20/crossing-over/

Hayes, Merdies. "Estevanico: The man, the myth, the legend." *Our Weekly Los Angeles*, 15 Feb. 2019, https://ourweekly.com/news/2019/02/15/estevanico-man-myth-legend/

Chapter 11: This Land is Your Land

This segment provided background about the history of the Navajo:

We Shall Remain the Navajo, *We Shall Remain: A Native History of Utah*, Produced by Jeff Elstad, PBS, 2009.

This piece contributed greatly to the chapter, especially regarding the NIYC's activism and the 1970s struggle against coal gasification:

Shreve, Bradley Glenn. "Up Against Giants: The National Indian Youth Council, the Navajo Nation, and Coal Gasification, 1974–77." *American Indian Culture and Research Journal*, vol. 30, no. 2, January 2006, pp. 17–34, https://meridian.allenpress.com/aicrj/article-abstract/30/2/17/210839/Up-against-Giants-The-National-Indian-Youth?redirectedFrom=fulltext

This interview provided the background and details about BMWC's activism:

Paget-Clarke, Nic. "Interview with Wahleah Johns and Lilian Hill Black Mesa Water Coalition." *In Motion Magazine*, 13 Jun. 2004, https://inmotionmagazine.com/global/wj_lh_int.html

These sources offered details about the history of extractive industries on Navajo lands:

Brynne Voyles, Traci. *Wastelanding: Legacies of Uranium Mining in Navajo Country*. University of Minnesota Press, 2015.

McPherson, Robert S. "Navajo Livestock Reduction in Southeastern Utah, 1933-46: History Repeats Itself." *American Indian Quarterly*, Volume 22, No 1/2, Winter-Spring 1998, pp. 1-18, https://www.jstor.org/stable/1185104?read-now=1&refreqid=excelsior%3A52372c36c2d311a27df687596c85e7bf&seq=7#page_scan_tab_contents

Thompson, Jonathan P. "How oil and greed led to the 1923 centralization of Navajo government." *The Land Desk*, 21 Dec. 2016, https://riveroflostsouls.com/2016/12/21/how-oil-and-greed-ledto-the-1923-centralization-of-navajo-government/

And this piece talks more about the push for Native-run renewable energy initiatives:

Johns, Wahleah. "Power Is in Our Hands: Native Renewables." Cooper Hewitt, 22 Apr. 2021, https://www.cooperhewitt.org/2021/04/22/power-is-in-our-hands/

Chapter 12: A Car in Every Garage

Articles that provided background on the history of highways and how America's dependence on cars was crafted:

Badger, Emily. "The myth of the American love affair with cars." *Washington Post*, 27 Jan. 2015, https://www.washingtonpost.com/news/wonk/wp/2015/01/27/debunking-the-myth-of-theamerican-love-affair-with-cars/

Fan, Yingling. "The Injustice and Sociopolitics of Transit Decline, 1921–1972." *Global Transit Blog*, 29 Mar. 2018, https://globaltransitblog.wordpress.com/2018/03/29/the-injustice-and-sociopoliticsof-transit-decline-1921-1972/

Herriges, Daniel. "The History of Urban Freeways: Who Counts?" Strong Towns, 21 Feb. 2017, https://www.strongtowns.org/journal/2017/2/20/the-history-of-urban-freeways-who-counts

Samuels, Alana. "The Role of Highways in American Poverty." *Atlantic*, 18 Mar. 2016, https://www.theatlantic.com/business/archive/2016/03/role-of-highways-in-american-poverty/474282/

Shill, Gregory H. "Americans Shouldn't Have to Drive, but the Law Insists on It." *Atlantic*, 9 Jul. 2019, https://www.theatlantic.com/ideas/archive/2019/07/car-crashes-arent-alwaysunavoidable/592447/

Stromberg, Joseph. "Highways gutted American cities. So why did they build them?" Vox, 11 May 2016, https://www.vox.com/2015/5/14/8605917/highways-interstate-cities-history

Wells, Christopher W. "Fueling the Boom: Gasoline Taxes, Invisibility, and the Growth of the American Highway Infrastructure, 1919–1956." *Journal of American History*, vol. 99, no. 1, Jun. 2012, pp. 72–81, https://academic.oup.com/jah/article/99/1/72/854562

CityLab's coverage of transportation and urban planning has deeply influenced my thinking, and both these pieces provided details and insight into contemporary freeway struggles (like the teen activists in Oregon):

Bliss, Laura. "The Road Warriors." CityLab, 22 Jan. 2022, https://www.bloomberg.com/news/features/2022-01-22/in-portland-youth-activists-are-driving-a-highway-revolt

Chu, Tiffany. "America's Transportation History is Full of Mistakes. Let's Not Make Another One." CityLab, 11 Sep. 2019, https://www.bloomberg.com/news/articles/2019-09-11/the-publicprivate-pathway-to-the-multimodal-city

Chapter 13: White Picket Fences

This was the piece that first introduced me to the history of SROs and inspired the original visual story I wrote for CityLab about the topic:

"History of S.R.O. Residential Hotels in San Francisco." Central City SRO Collaborative, http://www.ccsroc.net/s-r-o-hotels-in-san-francisco/

Books that go into great detail about residential hotels and hotel life:

Groth, Paul. *Living Downtown: The History of Residential Hotels in the United States*. University of

California Press, 1999.

Levander, Caroline Field, and Matthew Pratt Guterl. *Hotel Life: The Story of a Place Where Anything Can Happen*. University of North Carolina Press, 2015.

Articles about the SRO crisis and homelessness in New York City:

Berger, Joseph. "The Many Lives of a New York S.R.O." *New York Times*, 4 Jun. 2016, https://www.nytimes.com/2016/06/05/nyregion/the-many-lives-of-a-new-york-sro.html

Sullivan, Brian J., and Jonathan Burke. "Single-Room Occupancy Housing in New York City: The Origins and Dimensions of a Crisis." *The City University of New York Law Review*, vol. 17, no. 1, Winter 2013, https://academicworks.cuny.edu/cgi/viewcontent.cgi?article=1344&context=clr

"History of Supportive Housing." Supportive Housing Network of NY, https://shnny.org/supportivehousing/what-is-supportive-housing/history-of-supportive-housing/

"Why are so many people homeless?" Coalition for the Homeless, https://www.coalitionforthehomeless.org/why-are-so-many-people-homeless/

Articles about PHA and the work of housing activists in Philadelphia:

Baskin, Morgan. "Philadelphia Housing Authority Is Failing Unhoused Residents." *Philadelphia Inquirer*, 17 Jul. 2020, https://www.inquirer.com/opinion/commentary/philadelphia-housingauthority-encampments-homelessness-low-income-residents-20200717.html

Holder, Sara, and Brentin Mock. "A Group of Mothers, a Vacant Home, and a Win for Fair Housing." CityLab, 28 Jan. 2020, https://www.bloomberg.com/news/articles/2020-01-28/the-oakland-moms-who-launched-a-housing-movement

"Release: Philadelphia Housing Action Claims Victory After 6 Month Direct Action Campaign Forces City to Relinquish 50 Vacant Homes to Community Land Trust." Western Regional Advocacy Project, September 25, 2020, Press Release.

Chapter 14: Wish You Were Here

Haunani-Kay Trask's scholarship and activism was integral to this chapter, including:

Trask, Haunani-Kay. *From a Native Daughter: Colonialism and Sovereignty in Hawai'i*. University of Hawai'i Press, 1993.

Trask, Haunani-Kay. "The Struggle for Hawaiian Sovereignty." *Cultural Survival Quarterly Magazine*, Mar. 2000, https://www.culturalsurvival.org/publications/cultural-survival-quarterly/strugglehawaiian-sovereignty-introduction

Trask, Haunani-Kay. "Birth of the Modern Hawaiian Movement: Kalama Valley, O'ahu." *Hawaiian Journal of History*, vol. 21, 1987, https://evols.library.manoa.hawaii.edu/bitstream/10524/144/2/JL21142.pdf

Trask, Mililani, and Haunani-Kay Trask. "The Aloha Industry: For Hawaiian Women, Tourism Is Not a Neutral Industry." *Cultural Survival Quarterly Magazine*, Dec. 1992. https://www.culturalsurvival.org/publications/cultural-survival-quarterly/aloha-industry-hawaiian-womentourism-not-neutral-industry

This book has a detailed account of the US overthrow of Hawai'i's monarchy:

Kinzer, Stephen. *Overthrow: America's Century of Regime Change from Hawaii to Iraq*. Henry Holt and Company, 2006. 9780063140585

As does this article:

Dekneef, Matthew. "How White People Pushed Out Hawaiʻi's Monarchy." *Teen Vogue*, 25 Jan. 2019, https://www.teenvogue.com/story/how-white-people-pushed-out-hawaiis-monarchy

This is the article referenced on p. 187:

Curtis, Charlotte. "Where Aristocrats Do the Hula and Vote Republican." *New York Times*, 27 Nov. 1966, https://timesmachine.nytimes.com/timesmachine/1966/11/27/296400682. pdf?pdf_redirect=true&ip=0

For more about Hawaiian resistance:

Hofschneider, Anita. "Mauna Kea is the Latest in Long History of Native Hawaiian Protests." *Honolulu Civil Beat*, 30 Aug. 2019, https://www.civilbeat.org/2019/08/mauna-kea-is-the-latest-in-a-long-history-of-native-hawaiian-protests/

Kajihiro, Kyle. "Nation Under the Gun: Militarism and Resistance in Hawaiʻi." *Cultural Survival Quarterly Magazine*, Mar. 2000, https://www.culturalsurvival.org/publications/cultural-survival-quarterly/nation-under-gun-militarism-and-resistance-hawaii

And pieces about Hawaii's housing crisis:

Nagourney, Adam. "Aloha and Welcome to Paradise. Unless You're Homeless." *New York Times*, 3 Jun. 2016, https://www.nytimes.com/2016/06/04/us/hawaii-homeless-criminal-law-sittingban.html

Chang, William, and Abbey Seitz. "It's Time to Acknowledge Native Hawaiians' Special Right to Housing." *Honolulu Civil Beat*, 8 Jan. 2021, https://www.civilbeat.org/2021/01/its-time-to-acknowledge-native-hawaiians-special-right-to-housing/

Chapter 15: As American As

Julian Saporiti's music and work were a huge inspiration for this chapter, including:

For Joy. Written by Julian Saporiti, 2019, https://www.youtube.com/watch?v=ZU38Iw3Ec7k

"No-No Boy Julian Saporiti Says Music Is a Trojan Horse for Teaching Asian American History." *Here and Now*, hosted by Peter O'Dowd and Jeannette Muhammad, WBUR, 1 Apr. 2021, https://www.wbur.org/hereandnow/2021/04/01/no-no-boy-1975-julian-saporiti

Smithsonian Folkways Presents: No-No Boy—A Documentary on '1975.' Filmed by Albert Tong, Charlie Weber, and Julian Saporiti, 2021, https://www.youtube.com/

And I was introduced to Saporiti's music via this piece:

Zhang, Cat. "What is Asian American Music, Really?" Pitchfork, 31 May 2021, https://pitchfork.com/features/article/asian-american-music-history/

This article provided background about the George Igawa Orchestra:

Spitzer, Tanja B. "Music at Heart Mountain—The 'GI' Band That Crossed Borders." The National WWII Museum, 12 May 2021, https://www.nationalww2museum.org/war/articles/heart-mountain-George-igawa-orchestra

Details about life under internment came from these moving first-person accounts:

Inada, Lawson Fusao. *Only What We Could Carry: The Japanese American Internment Experience.* Heyday, 2014.

"Japanese Americans Interned During World War II." Telling Their Stories: Oral History Archives Project, https://www.tellingstories.org/internment/

"Prisoners at Home: Everyday Life in Japanese Internment Camps." Digital Public Library of America, https://dp.la/exhibitions/japanese-internment/road-camps

Chapter 16: The Old Ballgame

Dave Zirin's great work about Lester Rodney both introduced me to Rodney's story and provided the backbone for this chapter:

Zirin, Dave. "It All Starts with Lester Rodney." *What's My Name, Fool? Sports and Resistance in the United States.* Haymarket Books, 2005, pp. 23-36

Zirin, Dave. "Lester 'Red' Rodney: 1911–2009." *Nation*, 27 Dec. 2009, https://www.thenation.com/article/archive/lester-red-rodney-1911-2009/

There is also this interview with Rodney:

Attanasio, Ed. "The TGG Interview: Lester Rodney." *The Online Book of Baseball, This Great Game*, https://thisgreatgame.com/lester-rodney/

And Irwin Silber wrote a book about Rodney if you want to keep reading:

Silber, Irwin. *Press Box Red: The Story of Lester Rodney, the Communist Who Helped Break the Color Line in American Sports.* Temple University Press, 2003.

The following pieces provided more context about Jewish baseball players and Jewish support of Black players:

Lind, Dara. "The secret history of Jews in baseball." Vox, 2 Oct. 2014, https://www.vox.com/2014/10/2/6877671/the-secret-history-of-jews-in-baseball

Norwood, Stephen H. "Going to Bat for Jackie Robinson: The Jewish Role in Breaking Baseball's Color Line." *Journal of Sport History*, vol. 26, no. 1, Spring 1999, pp. 115-41, https://www.jstor.org/stable/43611720

And this Library of Congress exhibit has an overview of the history of baseball in the US and galleries of images:

Baseball Americana. 29 Jun. 2018–27 Jul. 2019, Library of Congress, Washington, DC, https://www.loc.gov/exhibitions/baseball-americana/about-this-exhibition/#explore-the-exhibit

Chapter 17: Down on the Farm

If you'd like to watch instead of read, there are a number of documentaries out there, including:

Delano Manongs: The Forgotten Heroes of the UFW. Directed by Marissa Aroy, 2014, https://vimeo.com/ondemand/delanomanongs?autoplay=1

Dolores. Directed by Peter Bratt, 2017, https://www.doloresthemovie.com/

Latino Americans, episode 5, "Prejudice and Pride." Series Producer Adriana Bosch, Editors David Espar and Manuel Tsingaris, PBS, 2013.

The Wrath of Grapes. United Farmworkers of America, 1987, https://www.youtube.com/watch?v=Wq48o4ftL4A

For more about Larry Itliong and the Filipino contribution to the strike:

Romasanta, Gayle. "Why It Is So Important to Know the Story of Filipino-American Larry Itliong." *Smithsonian Magazine*, 24 Jul. 2019, https://www.smithsonianmag.com/smithsonianinstitution/why-it-is-important-know-story-filipino-american-larry-itliong-180972696/

Articles and books that go into detail about what the strike was like:

Brimner, Larry Dane. *Strike! The Farm Workers' Fight for Their Rights*. Astra Publishing House, 2014.

Dunne, John Gregory. *Delano: The Story of the California Grape Strike*. University of California Press, 1967.

Garcia, Matt. "Cesar Chavez and the United Farmworkers Movement." *Oxford Research Encyclopedias*, 9 May 2016, https://oxfordre.com/americanhistory/view/10.1093/acrefore/9780199329175.001.0001/acrefore-9780199329175-e-217

Imutan, Andy. "When Mexicans and Filipinos Joined Together." United Farm Workers, Sept. 2005, https://ufw.org/mexicans-filipinos-joined-together/

Kim, Inga. "The Rise of the UFW." United Farm Workers, 3 Apr. 2017, https://ufw.org/the-rise-of-the-ufw/

Nelson, Eugene. *Huelga*. Farm Worker Press, 1966. https://libraries.ucsd.edu/farmworkermovement/essays/essays/HUELGA_Nelson.pdf

Go online to see galleries of incredible images (so many that I couldn't include in the book!) and more.

Chapter 18: Made in America

This book and article by Richard S. Newman provide detailed background about the history of Love Canal:

Newman, Richard S. *Love Canal: A Toxic History from Colonial Times to the Present*. Oxford University Press, 2016.

Newman, Richard S. "Making Love Canal: A Model City Turned Environmental Disaster." *Lapham's Quarterly*, 13 Jul. 2016, https://www.laphamsquarterly.org/roundtable/making-love-canal

Another great read about Niagara that includes the statistic about residents being offered $50 to make drums of waste disappear (p. 229):

Penner, Barbara. "Niagara: It Has It All." *Places*, Sept. 2009, https://placesjournal.org/article/niagara-it-has-it-all/

Interactive online exhibits that map toxic sites across the US:

"Toxic Sites." Brooke Singer, Lois Gibbs, John Kuiphoff, Matt Yu, https://www.toxicsites.us/

"Waste Land." KnightLab, David T. Hanson, 1985–1986, https://uploads.knightlab.com/storymapjs/3928f9055bedaff286ae87fbdbc4ff82/waste-land/index.html

Overview of the history of manufacturing and power in Niagara Falls:

Kowsky, Francis R., and Martin Wachadlo. *Historic Preservation Industrial Reconnaissance Survey: City of Niagara Falls, Niagara County, New York*. Niagara Falls Department of Community Development Office of Planning & Environmental Services, Nov. 2007, https://buffaloah.com/surveys/nfindustrial.html

More about the activism of residents at Love Canal (for a more comprehensive list of news articles from the time, including Michael Brown's reporting, go online):

Roth, Cassia. "For the Love of Data: Science, Protest, and Power at Love Canal." Nursing Clio, 11 May 2017, https://nursingclio.org/2017/05/11/for-the-love-of-data-science-protest-and-power-at-love-canal/

More recent investigations into the ongoing toxic legacy of Niagara Falls:

Tevlock, Dan. "Radioactive Hot Spots Pepper Niagara County." *Investigative Post*, 5 Jul. 2016, https://www.investigativepost.org/2016/07/05/radioactive-hot-spots-pepper-niagara-county/

Tevlock, Dan. "Landfill with Love Canal legacy still poses danger." *Investigative Post*, 10 Feb. 2016, https://www.investigativepost.org/2016/02/10/landfill-with-love-canal-legacy-still-posesdanger/

Depalma, Anthony. "A Toxic Waste Capital Looks to Spread It Around; Upstate Dump Is the Last in the Northeast." *New York Times*, 10 Mar. 2004, https://www.nytimes.com/2004/03/10/nyregion/toxic-waste-capital-looks-spread-it-around-upstate-dump-last-northeast.html

Chapter 19: Streets Paved with Gold

If you're intrigued by MLMs and want to learn more about their history, as well as listen to a nuanced exploration about why Americans are drawn to them, this podcast goes deep:

Marie, Jane. "Wanna Swim in Cash?" Produced by Witness Docs. *The Dream*, season 1, episode 1, 2018. Podcast.

Articles and first-person accounts that provide details about Amway:

Klebniov, Paul. "The Power of Positive Inspiration." *Forbes*, 9 Dec. 1991, https://skepdic.com/Klebniov.html

Scheibeler, Eric. *Merchants of Deception*. BookSurge, 2009.

Gerard, Sarah. "Going Diamond." *Granta*, 23 Nov. 2016, https://granta.com/going-diamond/

This piece provides background on LuLaRoe (and there is an associated documentary series you can watch):

Wilkinson, Alissa. "The Empty Dream that LuLaRoe Sold." Vox, 9 Sept. 2021, https://www.vox.com/22648447/lularich-lularoe-amazon-streaming

More about the perils of MLMs and how they operate:

Bond, Casey. "How MLMs and Cults Use the Same Mind Control Techniques." *Huffington Post*, 8 Jan. 2021, https://www.huffpost.com/entry/multilevel-marketing-companies-mlms-cults-similarities_l_5d49f8c2e4b09e72973df3d3

Multi-Level Marketing Businesses and Pyramid Schemes. Federal Trade Commission Consumer Advice, May 2021, https://consumer.ftc.gov/articles/multi-level-marketing-businesses-pyramid-schemes

"The Perils of Multi-Level Marketing Programs." *On Point*. Hosted by Tom Ashbrook, station, 4 Oct. 2017, https://www.tpr.org/2017-10-04/the-perils-of-multi-level-marketing-programs

Chapter 20: Nose to the Grindstone

This book provides a detailed history of Convict Leasing:

Blackmon, Douglas A. *Slavery by Another Name: The Re-Enslavement of Black Americans from the Civil War to World War II*. Anchor, 2008.

And this entry talks about it specifically in the context of Alabama:

Curtin, Mary Ellen. "Convict-Lease System." *Encyclopedia of Alabama*, 2007, http://encyclopediaofalabama.org/article/h-1346

This is the biography of John Henry that is referenced on p. 252:

Neslon, Scott Reynolds. *Steel Drivin' Man: John Henry The Untold Story of An American Legend*. Oxford University Press, 2006.

This is the article that provided the details about how laborers used the ballad of John Henry as they worked (p. 254):

Maxwell, Tom. "A History of American Protest Music: This Is the Hammer That Killed John Henry." Longreads, October 2017, https://longreads.com/2017/10/04/a-history-of-american-protest-music-this-is-the-hammer-that-killed-johnhenry/

This is the original ballad:

Anonymous. "John Henry." Poetry Foundation, https://www.poetryfoundation.org/poems/42897/john-henry

For more about modern day prison labor:

Singh, Maanvi. "California's Incarcerated Firefighters Face Dangerous Work, Low Pay and COVID-19." *High Country News*, 15 Jul. 2020, https://www.hcn.org/articles/climate-desk-wildfire-california-incarcerated-firefighters-face-dangerous-work-low-pay-and-covid19

Kamisher, Eliyahu. "Prison Labor Is on the Frontlines of the COVID-19 Pandemic" The Appeal, 5 Oct. 2020, https://theappeal.org/prison-labor-is-on-the-frontlines-of-the-covid-19-pandemic/

And an interview with Dr. Sherman James:

James, Sherman. "Sherman James on John Henryism." Social Science Space, 4 Aug. 2020, https://www.socialsciencespace.com/2020/08/sherman-james-on-john-henryism/

Chapter 21: We the People

This chapter was shaped by Iris Morales and Denise Oliver-Velez's powerful writing about their work with, and documentation of, the Young Lords:

Morales, Iris, and Denise Oliver-Velez. *The Young Lords: A Reader*. NYU Press, 2010.

Another brief history of the Young Lords:

Westcott, Jim. "A Brief History of the Young Lords." ThoughtCo., 20 Jun. 2018, https://www.thoughtco.com/young-lords-history-4165954

Newspaper articles about the Garbage Offensive and other Young Lords' initiatives:

Fried, Joseph P. "East Harlem Youths Explain Garbage-Dumping Demonstration." *New York Times*, 19 Apr. 1969, https://www.nytimes.com/1969/08/19/archives/east-harlem-youths-explain-garbage-dumping-demonstration.html

Older, Daniel José. "Garbage Fires for Freedom: When Puerto Rican Activists Took Over New York's Streets." *New York Times*, 11 Oct. 2019, https://www.nytimes.com/2019/10/11/nyregion/young-lords-nyc-garbage-offensive.html

Lubasch, Arnold H. "Young Lords Give Food and Care at Seized Church." *New York Times*, 30 Dec. 1969, https://www.nytimes.com/1969/12/30/archives/young-lords-give-food-and-care-at-seized-church.html

Narvez, Alfonso A. "The Young Lords Seize X-Ray Unit." *New York Times*, 18 Jun. 1970, https://www.nytimes.com/1970/06/18/archives/the-young-lords-seize-xray-unit-take-it-to-area-where-they-say-it.html

Martinez Sierra, Neyda. "Past Is Present: The Young Lords Party Revisited." The Latinx Project New York University, 15 Dec. 2021, https://www.latinxproject.nyu.edu/intervenxions/past-is-present-the-young-lords-party-revisited

For more about the mutual aid efforts mentioned at the end of the chapter as well as many more incredible images that I couldn't use, go online.

INDEX

Abbott, Sammie Abdullah, 155
abolitionists, 21, 24–33, 36–37
abortion, 73, 77, 79, 84
ACT UP, 86–97
Adams, Samuel, 102–4, 106
Adams, Sebastian C., 1–2
Adams' Synchronological Chart of Universal History (Adams, S. C.), 1
Agricultural Workers Organizing Committee, 215–21
AIDS epidemic, 84–97
Akwesasne Notes (newspaper), 57
Alabama, 14–15, 253
Albizu Campos, Don Pedro, 261
Amway, 240–44
Anthony, Susan B., 39
automobiles, 152–54, 158, 220
Al-Azemmouri, Mustafa "Estevanico," 124–31

Baker, Ella, 42
Baldwin, Marie Louise Bottineau, 41
"The Ballad of John Henry," 254–55
El Barrio, New York City, 258–62
baseball, color line, 204–11
Bayonet Constitution, 183, 184
Beck, Nancy B., 234
Bernard, Francis, 104
Best Families contest, 58–60
Black Codes, 9, 250–51
Black Mesa Water Coalition, 144–45, 147
Black Panthers, 16, 259, 261
bodily autonomy, 37, 67
Booker, Reginald H., 155
Boston, 24, 28, 100–106, 164
Brown, John, 28, 29, 31
Brown, Michael, 231
Brown v. Board of Education, 74
Burroughs, Nannie Helen, 40

Calhoun, John C., 11
Carlin, George, 237

Carter, Jimmy, 72–74, 80
Castle & Cooke, 179
Catlin, George, 115
Celler, Emanuel, 54, 55
Chavez, Cesar, 217–19
chemical companies, 229–35
Chicken Soup Brigade, 263
Chinese Exclusion Act, 49
Chisholm, Shirley, 43
Chuck D, 47
civil rights, 42, 141, 223, 261
Civil Rights Act, 75
Civil War, 8–9, 28, 32, 39, 116
Clark, Septima Poinsette, 42
climate change, 158–59
colonialism, 16, 140
color line, baseball, 204–11
Colt, Sam, 110–17
convict leasing, 250–54
Cooper, Anna Julia Haywood, 39
C&O Railroad, 252–53
Coronado, Francisco de, 124, 131
cotton, 23
COVID-19 pandemic, 45, 174

The Daily Worker (newspaper), 204–5, 207–8
Davis, Angela, 33
The Declaration of Sentiments, 38
De La Cruz, Iris, 95
Del Castillo Maldonado, Alonso, 127, 129
De Vaca, Alvar Núñez Cabeza, 126–29
Devos, Rich, 240, 245
DiMaggio, Joe, 207
Di Niza, Marcos, 130–31
disabled people, 44–45, 67, 90, 168
Dole, Sanford, 185
Dorantes de Carranza, Andrés, 127, 129–30
Douglass, Frederick, 16, 26–27
drugs, 88–89, 93–94, 96, 261
Du Bois, W. E. B., 16

Eisenhower, Dwight D., 153
Emergency Quota Act, 49, 52
energy production, 134–47
environment, 135–47, 223, 226, 229–35
equality, 16, 36–38, 73, 77
eugenics, 16, 59–67
Executive Order 9066, 194
extractive industries, 134–36, 138–47

Fair Play Committee, 199
Falwell, Jerry, 70–71, 73–80
Falwell, Jerry, Jr., 81
family, 58–60, 76
farmworkers, 43, 214–23
Fauci, Anthony, 88, 94
Fields, Mamie Garvin, 11
Filipinos, 166, 214–23
Fixico, Donald, 3
Four Corners region, 135
Free African Society, 262
freeway infrastructure, 153–59

The Garbage Offensive, 258–59
Garrison, William Lloyd, 28
gasification, 142–44
gender equality, 36–38, 73
genocide, 65, 180
Gibbs, Lois, 231
Gibson, Josh, 211
Gilmore, Ruth Wilson, 21
G.I. Orchestra, 196–97, 200
Graham, Billy, 240
Grant, Charlie, 211
grape strike, farmworkers, 214–23
Great Māhele Act, 181
Great Society Legislation, 43
Greenberg, Hank, 211
Greenfield, Elizabeth Taylor, 27
green jobs legislation, 145
Grimké sisters, 28
guns, 110–21

Hamer, Fannie Lou, 42, 63
Harding, Warren G., 48–49
Harper, Frances Ellen Watkins, 38, 39

Harpers Ferry, 28
Hart-Celler Act, 54–55
Hartman, Saidiya V., 247
Haslip, Katrina, 95
Haudenosaunee women, 37
Hawai'i, 177, 179–89
Heart Mountain, 196–200
Henry, John, 248–49, 252, 254–55
Hernández, Antonia, 64
history, 1–5, 7, 14–16, 18–19, 261
Hitler, Adolf, 53, 61
Hooker Chemicals, 230–31
Hoover Dam, 138
Hoth, Dan, 93
housing, 162–75, 178–79, 188–89, 231
Huerta, Dolores, 43, 213, 217, 219

Igawa, George, 196–97, 200
"I Love America" rallies, 70–71, 78, 84
immigration, 42, 49–55, 67, 262
incarceration camps, 194–200
informed consent, 62, 65, 67
International Longshore and Warehouse Union,
    220
Itliong, Larry, 216–19, 223

Jackson, Andrew, 22
Jacobs, Jane, 154
James, Sherman, 255
Japanese Americans, 186, 192–200
Jews, 53, 166, 209, 211, 262
Johns, Wahleah, 147
Johnson-Reed Act, 52–54
Joncaire, Daniel, 228
Jones, Bob, 84
Jordan, June, 257
"Journal of Occurrences," 101–2
justice, 8, 140–41, 143–45, 147, 159

Kahn, Roger, 209
Kansas Free Fair, 58–60
Keller, Helen, 40
King, Martin Luther, Jr., 69, 75
Ku Klux Klan, 9, 14

labor, 43, 73, 138–39, 145–46, 182, 262
    convict leasing, 250–54
    grape strike, 214–23
    women and, 38, 40, 41, 167, 239
labyrinths, 267–68
Laduke, Winona, 140
land
    Hawai'i, 177, 179–86, 189
    Native Americans, 22–23, 57, 114, 135–47,
    194
Laughlin, Harry, 52
Lee, Mabel Ping-Hua, 41
Le Guin, Ursula K., 203
Leonard, Zoe, 97
LGBTQ, 44, 73, 263
The Liberator (newspaper), 28
Lili'uokalani (Queen of Hawai'i), 184–85
Lloyd, John Henry, 211
The Lost Cause, 12
Love Canal, toxic waste, 230–33
loyalty questionnaire, 198–200
LuLaRoe, 244

Manifest Destiny, 1, 114
McCloud, Janet, 43
Means, Lorelei Decora, 43
"A Measuring Rod" pamphlet, 13
Mendoza y Pacheco, Antonio de, 129, 130
Mexican braceros, 43, 214, 217–23
military, 32, 118–20, 179, 182–86, 189, 198–200
mining, 138, 146, 232, 253
Mink, Patsy Takemoto, 43
missionaries, in Hawai'i, 180–82, 184, 186–87
Morales, Iris, 263–65
Moral Majority, 76–78, 80–81, 84–85
Morrison, Jim, 99
Morrison, Toni, 123
Moses, Robert, 154
multi-level marketing, 238–45
Murray, Pauli, 35

Narváez expedition, 126–29
National Farm Workers Association, 217–21
National Indian Youth Council, 133, 141,
    143–44

National Institutes of Health (NIH), 89–94
National Interstate and Defense Highways Act,
    153
"national sacrifice zone," 135
Native Americans, 3, 41–43, 62, 65, 133, 261
    Haudenosaunee women, 37
    land, 22–23, 57, 114, 135–47, 194
    tribal groups, 2, 22, 57, 118, 129, 131, 135–
    39, 142–47, 262, 267
Native Renewables, 147
Negro Leagues, baseball, 206–7
Newsome, Bree, 19
New York City, 19, 24, 26, 30, 154, 209
    El Barrio, 258–62
    housing, 164, 166, 168, 170–73
New York Times (newspaper), 19
Niagara Falls, 226–33, 235
NIH (National Institutes of Health), 89–94
Nixon, Richard, 134–35
No-No Boys, 200

Obama, Barack, 55
Occupy PHA, 174–75
The Old-Time Gospel Hour, 70, 78–79
Oliver-Velez, Denise, 263–65

Padilla, Gilbert, 217
Paige, Satchel, 207, 211
Paul Bunyan (fictional character), 248
Peabody Western Coal Company, 139, 142,
    144–45
Pearl Harbor, 179, 186, 192
Pecos Bill (fictional character), 248
petroglyphs, 267
Petty, Tom, 149
Pinkerton-Uri, Constance Redbird, 65
plantations, 12, 14–15, 23, 179, 181–82, 184,
    186–87, 189
police, 26, 31, 33, 120, 217, 250–51
politics, 48–49, 71–81, 84–85, 96, 223
pollution, 158, 226, 229–35
Povich, Shirley, 209
prisons, 33, 60, 62, 67, 194–200, 250–54
Puerto Rico, 64, 261
pyramid schemes, 243–44

racism, 8–16, 18–19, 29, 33, 39, 255, 262
    baseball and color line, 204–11
    Japanese Americans and, 186, 192–200
    urban renewal and, 154–57, 159
Reagan, Ronald, 55, 79–81, 85, 221
Reciprocity Treaty, 182
redlining, 154
Reed, David A., 50, 52, 53
religion, politics and, 71–81, 84–85
Robinson, Jackie, 210–11
Rodney, Lester, 205, 207–9, 211
Rodríguez Trías, Helen, 64
Roe v. Wade, 73
Roosevelt, Franklin D., 194
Rosenfeld, Bernard, 64
Ruggles, David, 26, 31
Russell, Lillian, 48–52, 55
Russo, Vito, 83
Rutherford, Mildred Lewis, 13

Saporiti, Julian, 191, 200–201
Schneiderman, Rose, 40, 41
Schoellkopf, Joseph, 228
schools, 65, 73–75, 79, 121, 260–61
Seeger, Pete, 220
Seneca Falls Convention, 38
Seven Cities of Cibola, 129, 130, 131
Shipwrecked (De Vaca), 126–29
shootings, mass, 121
single-room occupancy, 168–73
1619 Project, New York Times, 19
slavery, 19, 23, 107, 182, 247
    abolitionists and, 24–33, 36
    supporters, 11–12, 14–16
Smith, Joseph, 244
solar power, 147
Stamp Act, 103
Standing Rock, 147
Stanton, Elizabeth Cady, 38, 39
sterilization, of women, 61–67
Stevens, John L., 185
Stidham, Mark, 244
"Storm the NIH" action, 89–94
Student Nonviolent Coordinating Committee,
    42

sugar, 103, 182, 186, 187
Sunrise Movement, 159
Superfund sites, 140, 231, 232
Supreme Court, 22, 74, 75

Takeshita, Joy, 197
textbooks, 3–4, 12–16, 18–19, 77
300-mile march action, 220
Thunder Hawk, Madonna, 43
Thurston, Lorrin, 184–85
Torrey, Charles Turner, 28, 29, 31
tourism, 179, 187, 188, 235
Townshend Acts, 100, 103
toxic waste, 226, 229–35
Trask, Haunani-Kay, 177
Treaty of Bosque Redondo, 137
Trump, Donald, 55, 81, 234
Truth, Sojourner, 32
Tubman, Harriet, 32
Twain, Mark, 7

UDC (United Daughters of the Confederacy),
    8–14, 19
Underground Railroad, 26
unhoused, 172, 174–75, 178–79
United Auto Workers, 220
United Daughters of the Confederacy (UDC),
    8–14, 19
United Farmworkers of America, 220–22
urban renewal, 154–57, 159
Utah International, 139, 142

violence, 25, 27–28, 30–31, 40, 42, 105–6, 139
voting, 36, 39–45, 48, 79, 183–84

Walker, David, 27
Walker, Sam, 111
Washington Metro System, 155
water, 135, 139, 142, 144–45, 147, 189, 227–29
Wells, Ida B., 40
Weyrich, Paul, 74, 76
white supremacy, 8–16, 18, 19
Winchell, Walter, 209
women, 92, 94–95, 166, 174–75, 244, 262
    Haudenosaunee, 37

labor and, 38, 40, 41, 167, 239
    sterilization of, 61–67
    UDC and white, 8–14, 19
    voting rights for, 36, 39–45, 48
Wong, Alice, 45
World War II, 119, 168, 186

Young, Phyllis, 43
The Young Lords, 258–65
Youth vs. ODOT, 159

Zitkála-Šá, 41